The Idylls of Theokritos

The Idylls

of

Theokritos

a verse translation
by Barriss Mills

Purdue University Studies
West Lafayette, Indiana

Fifth printing, December 1972

A slightly different version of the Eleventh *Idyll*
appeared in *Sparrow,* No. 16, December, 1961.

PREFACE

IT has not been my intention to produce a new reading of the *Idylls*. That is work for Greek scholars, and I am not one. What's more, it has been done, recently and definitively, by A. S. F. Gow, whose handsome edition of the Greek text includes an excellent prose translation. To know as nearly as possible what Theokritos wrote, we must turn to Gow, whether we read Greek or not. But where the text is corrupt, or its sense dubious, I have ventured my own unscholarly guesses as to what the poet may have had in mind.

My purpose has been to write modern English verse which reflects the spirit and tone of the *Idylls*. I have found that this can best be accomplished by a fairly literal rendering, with allowance for the differences between Greek and English idiom and between English verse and prose.

Most verse translations of Theokritos have used one or another accentual meter thought to be comparable to the Greek hexameters. The most successful recent attempt along these lines is R. C. Trevelyan's version, written in unrhymed lines of seven beats. But the demands of regular meter, coupled with a decision to translate line by line, force him into alternate contraction and padding out of the lines, as well as a good many inversions of normal English word order. My own choice has been a not too strict syllabic meter, varying from a norm of seven or eight syllables in the line to a norm of eleven or twelve syllables, depending upon the character of each idyll. I have abandoned the line-by-line approach except where it was necessary to preserve the stichomythic pattern in certain idylls. The reader may judge whether the gain in freedom for a natural, idiomatic English is worth the sacrifice of a more insistent metrical pattern. I shall be content if I have succeeded in making of each idyll a readable, modern English poem which does justice to Theokritos' luminous imagery, his subtle characterization, and his anti-heroic humor and irony.

v

My use of the Greek forms of proper names, even when the Latin or English forms are more familiar, is not mere pedantry. Theokritos relies heavily upon proper names for effects of sound as well as "color," and such spellings as "Kyklops" and "Kirke" and "Aigyptos" and "Neilos," though they may look strange, seem to me to preserve the flavor of what Theokritos wrote better than their Latinized or Anglicized equivalents.

I must acknowledge my debt to other translators—particularly to Gow and Trevelyan, but also to earlier translators like Andrew Lang and the Rev. J. Banks. From all of them I have borrowed freely, on the assumption that translating, like dictionary-making, is a "cumulative" art.

I should like to express my thanks to Marbury Bladen Ogle, formerly chairman of the Department of Classics at the University of Minnesota, for his help at several difficult points. Had he been able to read the entire manuscript, this would be a better translation. But the person who has helped me most, at every stage, is my wife, Iola J. Mills.

—Barriss Mills

West Lafayette, Indiana
October 1, 1962

The Poetry of Theokritos

PASTORAL is a minor genre. It speaks with a deliberately less
heroic voice than epic, and it does not attempt the large dissonances
and harmonies of tragedy. Beside them, it may seem a frivolous sort of
poetry, inviting us to forget for awhile man's destiny and man's fate
to indulge ourselves in a daydream of rustic simplicity and romantic
love.

The range of pastoral is limited. We hear the full gamut in
Theokritos, who invented the form, and it quickly becomes shrill or
cloying in his immediate followers, Bion and Moschos. Later imitators,
beginning with Vergil and continuing spasmodically down to the 18th
century, turned it into a literary convention, stiff and lifeless and dull.
And when Marie Antoinette put on a shepherdess's costume to lead
picnics into the French countryside, pastoral breathed its last faint
breath and died.

But in the *Idylls* we have pastoral still fresh and fluid and vigorous.
We hear Theokritos trying out the possibilities of his new poetic instru-
ment and coloring each poem with his own vocal timbre. If he remains
a minor poet, it is because the genre he fashioned is a minor one, not
because his talents are inferior. "Major" and "minor" are terms dear
to critics and literary historians. In the world of poetry itself there are
only good poets and bad, and Theokritos is one of the best.

The simplicity of pastoral is deceptive. It does not exist, ready-made,
in nature, or we should not have had to wait till the early decades of
the third century B.C. for its discovery. It is an artful simplicity,
contrived by a poet of great skill. It is also a by-product of one of the
most complex and artificial periods of Greek culture, the age of defeatism
and disillusion between the fall of Athens in the Peloponnesian War
and the coming of the Romans.

Pastoral offered a romantic escape from the *fin-de-siècle* mood of the
hellenistic period. It came into being when the prevailing art and culture
had become far enough removed from the real life of countrymen for
its hardships and difficulties to be almost forgotten, and it presented
the charms of rustic life in learned, polished verse aimed at a sophisticated, urban audience.

The Idylls of Theokritos

The ambiguous nature of pastoral is revealed quite clearly in the seventh idyll. Here we find the most lyrical description of nature any-where in Theokritos. But this rustic paradise is seen through the eyes of city men going to the harvest festival for a holiday, to rest their bodies and minds for awhile in nature's beauty and bounty—not unpro-vided with well-aged wine.

We move further into the pastoral world in the other bucolic idylls, which are inhabited by herdsmen and other rustics. There we have, full-blown, the fantasy of a leisurely life in the midst of a gentle and beneficent nature, where the chief occupation is singing and piping and the only threat to peace of mind is unsatisfied love. Presented by a less skillful poet, such a world might seem not only unbelievable but vapid. And so it does seem, in the hands of later pastoralists. But Theokritos never forgets he is creating a fantasy, never takes his own fiction too seriously, and never fails to provide us with clues as to the relation of his imaginary scenes and characters to the real world.

In the tenth idyll, Milon's realistic view of the farmer's life makes Boukaios' lovesickness seem a bit ridiculous, and Boukaios' charmingly clumsy love-song for Bombyka sustains the mood of gentle irony. In the twenty-first, Asphalion's dream of the golden fish is offset by his friend's down-to-earth view of the fisherman's lot. In other bucolic idylls we find the romantic, almost sentimental attitude toward nature and love balanced by frequent horseplay and rough joking.

One of the things that keep the *Idylls* fresh and believable is a way of looking at his characters and their actions which is almost as original with Theokritos as his formulation of pastoral. We may call it "psycho-logical" or "dramatic," but an even better term, if we permit ourselves to skip over several centuries of literary history, is "novelistic." It is characterized by an insistence upon looking at experience through the minds of his characters in addition to seeing them from the outside as "types." Much of the humor and irony of the *Idylls* comes from the persistent use of such "double vision," and the occasions where it is lacking — notably the twenty-third and twenty-sixth idylls — produce Theokritos' least attractive poems.

A good example is the third idyll, in which the young goatherd pleads in vain with Amaryllis to come out of her cave and let him kiss her. Being a very young lover, he worries about his own appearance, tries to bribe the girl with apples, envies the bees who can penetrate her cave, threatens suicide, reveals his superstitious belief in "signs," compares himself with legendary herdsmen who have been successful in love, teases her about her lack of initiation into certain cult mysteries, and throws himself down, in an orgy of self-pity, for the wolves to eat.

The poem is both a case history of adolescent love and a charming dramatization of the young man's moods. We can smile at him and sympathize with him at once.

Similarly, Polyphemos in the eleventh idyll rings the changes on the theme of the pleading lover, alternating between cajolery of Galateia and pity for himself. But the one-eyed giant also reveals himself as a clumsy, rather stupid fellow, unable to sustain the proper romantic tone. His head and feet ache, as well as his heart, and he will complain to his mother about it. His lovesickness is absurd, yet somehow we are made to believe in it and to share his feelings.

The tour-de-force of such double vision is the second idyll, in which Simaitha is shown alternating between hatred of Delphis for having deserted her and the vain hope that he will return. Even her black magic seems intended both to punish him and bring him back to her. No modern novelist or short-story writer has dealt more convincingly with the moods of a jilted woman. We know, as she sometimes does, that this has been a typical seduction and desertion. Yet Simaitha's story is individualized by such charming touches as her pleasure in a new dress, her constant worry about her beauty, and her pathetic eagerness to swallow Delphis' "line," even though she knows it is one. In this idyll the "double vision" is operative not only for the poet and reader but for Simaitha herself, and we are reminded of the complexities of comic characterization in the heroines of Shakespeare's romantic comedies.

Psychology spills over into social satire in the fourteenth and fifteenth idylls. The fourteenth gives us a quickly drawn but incisive picture of Aischines' wine-party at his country place, his sudden quarrel with Kyniska, and his melodramatic performance as a forlorn lover afterward. Because Aischines is quite clearly a sophisticated man-about-town, and because he is overacting, we are less inclined to sympathize with him than to laugh at him, along with Thyonichos. Knowing this, Theokritos shifts the focus of the poem at the end to praise of Ptolemy, and Aischines' troubles are forgotten.

The famous fifteenth idyll sketches a brilliant, brittle picture of two Syrakousan ladies chattering together in Praxinoa's suburban house and marveling with provincial awe at the crowded streets of Alexandria and the sentimental Adonis tableau and dirge-singing at the Ptolemies' *nouveau-riche* palace. The women are silly, but Theokritos does not moralize about their silliness. In fact, he makes it quite appealing, and he individualizes Praxinoa's light-mindedness far beyond anything in the other "mimes" of the period or even in the New Comedy of Menander.

We have moved a long way from bucolic pastoral in this idyll set in the new metropolis Alexander had built at the mouth of the Nile.

The two giddy ladies, who might well be wives of minor officials in the court bureaucracy, are much too citified to concern themselves with goats and pastures and rustic songs. But they do talk about babies, dressmaking, and the shortcomings of husbands, and they seem as blissfully unaware of wars and politics as the herdsmen in the bucolic idylls. This is urban pastoral, a contradiction in terms only if we insist that pastoral deal exclusively with rustic life. A broader definition of pastoral as the deliberate turning of attention from the larger issues to the minutiae of daily life will encompass the fourteenth and fifteenth idylls as well as the bucolic ones and will more accurately describe the range of Theokritos' poetry.

Such a definition will also describe Theokritos' poetic strategy in the "epic" idylls. There the traditional stories of Herakles are "modernized" by a rather violent shifting of focus away from the heroic aspects of the legend to its potentialities for a more "intimate," casual treatment. In the thirteenth idyll, the epic purpose of the Argo's cruise is forgotten not only by Herakles but by the poet and reader, as attention is centered on the capture of Hylas by the water-nymphs and Herakles' subsequent grief. In the twenty-fourth idyll, the strangling of the serpents by the infant Herakles is shifted from the center of the poem to its beginning and disposed of quickly and rather undramatically so that attention may dwell upon the domestic arrangements of Alkmena's household and the schooling of young Herakles.

There is a more complicated skewing of traditional epic values in the long twenty-fifth idyll. We are led by the opening scenes to expect an account of one of Herakles' famous labors—the cleansing of the Augeian stables. But though we are taken on an inspection tour of the stables and pastures, and see the herds pouring in at evening over the plain, there is never any mention of that task. Instead, a new pattern is set up, with the dogs barking at Herakles in the first part of the poem, the prize bull, Phaethon, charging against him in the second part, and Herakles' own rather modest account of the attack of the Nemean lion upon him and his slaying of it, at the end of the idyll. Thus we are finally told of one of Herakles' labors, but not the one we had been promised. Theokritos is slyly crossing (or, more accurately, double-crossing) the expectations which epic has set up. He is turning the Herakles legend upside down and inside out in order to breathe new life into a story that has been told too often. In all these idylls, the fabulous Dorian hero is brought down from the status of a demi-god to the more appealing status of a boy and man, though an unusually strong and brave one.

Something comparable happens to those other demi-gods, the Dioskouri, in the twenty-second idyll. The poem begins as a hymn, with an invocation of the heavenly twins, a Homeric description of a ship in a storm at sea, and an epic account of the disembarkation from the *Argo* and the discovery of the spring and the giant Amykos. But suddenly the style of the poem changes. Polydeukes and Amykos engage in sticho-mythic repartee reminiscent of the bucolic idylls, and we are given a realistic, blow-by-blow account of the boxing match much as it might be narrated by a radio announcer today. The hymn form is abandoned for story-telling, and Polydeukes is reduced from a divinity to a man.

A more remarkable reversal of epic values occurs in the second episode of this idyll—the sword-fight between Kastor and Lynkeus. In the first episode Amykos is a bully, and we are on the side of Polydeukes as he cuts the giant to pieces with his thonged fists. But in the second episode it is the heroic twins who are trouble-makers, stealers of other men's betrothed wives, and it is Lynkeus who delivers the long con-ciliatory speech pleading for a settlement of the quarrel through friend-ship and reason rather than force. Kastor's only answer is to slaughter Lynkeus with his sword, and our sympathies are with the sons of Aphareus rather than the Dioskouri.

Troubled by this, some scholars have hypothesized a passage now lost from the poem in which the speaker becomes Kastor rather than Lynkeus, in order to credit Kastor with the plan for reducing the carnage. But nothing in the text supports that supposition, and we must reject it as a product of wishful thinking and an embarrassed sense of the epic proprieties on the part of the scholars. But Theokritos cared nothing for epic proprieties. He is deliberately flaunting them in this idyll by turning one of his heroes into a bully and presenting one of his heroes' victims in a noble light. This is the sort of transvaluation of epic values of which Theokritos is quite capable. And his distaste for the Dioskouri's part in the quarrel with Aphareus' sons is in keeping with a dislike of warfare which we see here and there in the other idylls. The dominant mood of pastoral is peace and friendship and love, not adven-turousness and fighting.

The bucolic element in pastoral attains its fullest development in the first idyll. Daphnis' lament is the archetype of all the love-songs in the idylls. There is something mythical about it, comparable at the pastoral level with the myths of the Olympian gods and Homeric heroes which Theokritos treats so lightly. This is suggested by the great length of the lament and by its refrain which invokes the Muses. There is also some-thing curiously vague and unreal about Daphnis' lovesickness and dying. We are never quite sure what his trouble is, or why it must end in death. He seems not to be suffering from the usual pastoral complaint—unrequited love. Indeed, we are led to believe that the girl he loves is wandering somewhere in an equally forlorn state, yearning for him. The explanation seems to be that he has taken a vow of chastity which he can keep only by giving up the ghost. In the romantic atmosphere of pastoral, such a militant refusal to submit to love's blandishments produces a *lusus naturae*. Even the gods and animals stand in awe of such heroic chastity. And we should be inclined to scoff at it if Theokritos had not forestalled us by providing at the beginning of the idyll one of his "clues" to the relation of myth and reality—the description of the bowl Thyrsis is to receive in payment for his song.

The long description of the bowl seems on first thought to throw the structure of the idyll out of balance. It delays the action, and it sets up a different mood from that of the Daphnis song. For the bowl, unlike the Daphnis story, is insistently real—so clearly seen, and smelled, as to seem almost tangible. Our attention is divided between two centers of interest and two different "tones," and absolute unity of effect is lost. And yet the imagistic description of the bowl is needed in the poem. It offsets the vagueness of the Daphnis story. It keeps our mind in part on the real world of people and nature and animals, while the Daphnis story pulls us in the direction of the mythical side of pastoral.

The architecture of the *Idylls* is not the classical symmetry of Greek temples or vases. It takes dangerous leaps, seems to lose its balance, and recovers by a leap in another, often unexpected direction. It is a dynamic, kinetic architecture, like that of Shakespeare's plays or the modern novel.

The delicate balance between reality and myth which Theokritos created in the *Idylls* was never attained again, except perhaps in Shakespeare. Vergil's pastoral is more polished, more decorous, more serene, and some have preferred it. Indeed, a preference for Vergil's pastoral over Theokritos' is one of the touchstones of neo-classical criticism. But romantics have just as consistently preferred Theokritos, and I do not hesitate to enroll myself under their banner on this issue. Beside that of Theokritos, Vergil's pastoral seems to me pale and formal, "literary," almost academic.

Theokritos almost makes us believe in his pastoral world. He has seen and smelled the Sicilian countryside, and heard the insects at high noon. He names with their real names the flowers and trees and grasses, and he knows the seasons when different flowers bloom and fruits ripen. He has heard the rude singing-matches between Sicilian peasants which he transforms into poetry in the bucolic idylls, and he has known the "originals" of the rustics who people them, subtly individualized and differentiated from one another. He knows something of spinning, something of weaving, something of chariot-making (the image, in the twenty-fifth idyll, of the figwood wheel-rim springing from the workman's hand is one of his best), something of folk-magic and country superstitions.

All these things are transmuted in the *Idylls*. They take on a luminous quality when fused in the pastoral myth. But Theokritos starts with reality as he has known it, not with a dusty literary convention. And he proceeds with almost perfect taste to make something fresh and lyrical of these ingredients. His is not the "good taste" of the literary drudge or petty critic—that deadly "good taste" which insists upon "rules" and the fashionable mixture as before. His is the instinctive taste of the original artist who combines new and unexpected things into patterns that somehow hold together and enable us to see the world in a new way.

He dares to begin his epithalamion for Menelaos and Helen with a broad joke and end it with a paean to conjugal love. He dares to refer, in his open appeal for a patron, to the rejected poems huddled away in the bottom of a trunk. He dares, in short, to make charming poetry of the incongruities and absurdities of experience as well as its moments of sweetness and beauty. The stuffier critics and literary historians will never forgive him for this.

FIRST IDYLL

Thyrsis. The whispering of that pinetree by the spring
is sweet music, goatherd, and your piping
is sweet too. You'll take the second prize
after Pan. If he chooses the horned goat,
you'll get the she. But if he's awarded
the she-goat, the kid will come to you.
And kids' flesh is sweet before you milk them.

Goatherd. Shepherd, your song is sweeter than the water
that tumbles and splashes down from the rocks.
If the Muses get the ewe for their prize,
you'll win the sucking lamb. But if they choose
the lamb, you'll carry away the ewe.

Thyrsis. In the Nymphs' name, goatherd, won't you sit down
on this slope among the tamarisks
and pipe, while I look after your goats?

Goatherd. No, shepherd. We never pipe at noon,
for fear of Pan, who's resting then,
tired from the chase. His temper's short,
and bitter anger quivers on his nostrils.
But Thyrsis, you used to sing of Daphnis'
troubles, and you're skilled in pastoral song.
Let's sit under that elm, facing the statue
of Priapos and the Nymphs of the Spring,
over where the shepherds' seat and the oak trees are.
And if you'll sing as you did against Chromis,
the Libyan, I'll let you milk three times
a she-goat that's borne twins and when she's suckled them
yields two pailfuls besides. And I'll give you
a deep bowl too, rubbed with sweet wax,
double-handled, newly carved, still smelling
from the chisel. Along the upper lip
runs ivy intertwined with marigold.

1

All around it winds a tendril
proud with its yellow fruit. And inside
is fashioned a woman such as the gods
might make, dressed in a robe and snood.
And beside her two handsome, long-haired men
contend with one another in talking,
yet her heart is untouched. She glances
at one of them and smiles, but her thoughts
are on the other, while their eyes
are hollow with longing, but in vain.
Beside them is shown an old fisherman
and a jagged rock on which the old man
busily gathers his great net for a cast
like a man that puts his heart in his work.
You'd say he was fishing with all the strength
of his limbs, the way the muscles stand out
about his neck. And though he's gray-haired,
he has the strength of youth. And not far
from the sea-battered old man is a vineyard,
loaded with red-ripe clusters and guarded
by a small boy sitting on a stone wall.
On either side of him are two foxes.
One goes up and down the vine-rows, stealing
the ripe grapes, while the other concentrates
all her cunning on the boy's leather bag,
vowing she'll never let him alone
till she's made away with his breakfast.
But the boy weaves a pretty cricket-cage
of asphodel bound round with rushes,
and takes more pleasure in his weaving
than care for his wallet and his vines.
And around the bowl in all directions
winds the supple acanthus, a marvel
of craftsmanship, something to wonder at.
I paid a ferryman of Kalydon
a goat and a great white cheese for it.
But it's still new, and has never yet
touched my lips. I'll give it to you
gladly, friend, if you'll sing me that fine song.
And I mean what I say. Begin, good sir,
for you mustn't save up your singing
for Haides, where everything's forgotten.

Thyrsis sings: *Begin the song, dear Muses.*
Begin the pastoral song.

Thyrsis of Aitna am I,
and sweet is the voice of Thyrsis.
Where were you, Nymphs, where were you
when Daphnis was wasting with love?
In Peneios' lovely valley?
Or Pindos'? Surely it wasn't
the great river of Anapos,
nor Aitna's peak, nor the holy
stream of Akis that held you.

Begin the song, dear Muses.
Begin the pastoral song.

The jackals howled for him,
and the wolves. Even the lion
of the forest wept for him dead.

Begin the song, dear Muses.
Begin the pastoral song.

At his feet many cattle,
and many bulls, and many
heifers and calves lamented.

Begin the song, dear Muses.
Begin the pastoral song.

First Hermes came from the hill
and said "Daphnis, who torments you?
Friend, who is it you love so much?"

Begin the song, dear Muses.
Begin the pastoral song.

The cowherds came, and the shepherds
and the goatherds came and asked
what ailed him. And Priapos
came and said "Poor Daphnis,
why are you wasting? For you
an unbedded girl wanders
by every spring and grove—

Begin the song, dear Muses.
Begin the pastoral song.

searching. You're a foolish lover
and a feeble one. You're called

3

cowherd, but you're behaving
more like the goatherd who watched
the she-goats skipping and wept
because he wasn't a goat.

Begin the song, dear Muses.
Begin the pastoral song.

And you, when you see girls laughing,
weep because you aren't dancing
among them." The cowherd made
no answer, but endured
his bitter love—endured it
to his predestined end.

Begin the song again, Muses.
Begin the pastoral song.

And then Kypris came to him,
smiling, hiding her anger
with a crafty smile, and said
"You vowed you'd give Love a fall,
Daphnis, but haven't you instead
been thrown by cruel Love?"

Begin the song again, Muses.
Begin the pastoral song.

This time Daphnis answered her:
"Cruel Kypris, vengeful Kypris,
Kypris hated by mortals,
do you think all my suns have set?
Even in Haides, Daphnis
will be an enemy of Love.

Begin the song again, Muses.
Begin the pastoral song.

Don't they tell of Kypris
and the cowherd? Get yourself
to Ida, back to Anchises.
There are oaks and sedge, and bees
hum sweetly about the hives.

Begin the song again, Muses.
Begin the pastoral song.

Adonis too is young.
He herds his sheep, shoots rabbits,
and hunts all the wild beasts.

Begin the song again, Muses.
Begin the pastoral song.
Go present yourself again
to Diomedes and say
'I'm victor over Daphnis,
the cowherd. Come fight with me.'
Begin the song again, Muses.
Begin the pastoral song.
Farewell, you wolves and jackals
and bears in your mountain caves.
Your herdsman Daphnis will come
no more to your woods and groves.
Farewell, too, Arethousa,
and you other rivers that pour
your lovely waters down Thybris.
Begin the song again, Muses.
Begin the pastoral song.
I am Daphnis that herded
his cattle here and watered
his bulls here and his calves.
Begin the song again, Muses.
Begin the pastoral song.
O Pan, Pan, whether
you're in Lykaios' tall hills
or herd on high Mainalos,
come to Sikelia's island
and leave the peak of Helike
and the upland tomb of the son
of Lykaon, which even
the blessed ones delight in.
Come finish the song, Muses.
Finish the pastoral song.
Come, master, and take this pipe,
smelling of honey from the wax
well moulded round its lip,
for Love calls me now to Haides.
Come finish the song, Muses.
Finish the pastoral song.
Bear violets, you brambles,
and you thorns, bear violets.
Narcissus bloom on juniper,

and everything grow askew.
Let the pinetrees grow pears
now that Daphnis is dying.
Let the stag harry the hounds,
and the owls upon the hills
outsing the nightingales."

Come finish the song, Muses.
Finish the pastoral song.

Saying this, he made an end.
Aphrodite would have raised him
once more, but the thread of the Fates
was all run out, and Daphnis
crossed over the stream. The flood
covered him the Muses loved
and the Nymphs did not dislike.

Come finish the song, Muses.
Finish the pastoral song.

Now give me the goat and bowl,
and I will milk her and make
libation to the Muses.
Farewell and always farewell,
Muses, and someday I
will sing you a better song.

Goatherd. May your lovely mouth be filled with honey,
Thyrsis, and with honeycomb. And may you eat
sweet figs from Aigilos, for your singing
is better than the cicada's. Here's the bowl.
Notice, friend, how good it smells. You'd think
it had been dipped in the well of the Hours.
Come, Kissaitha! Now milk her. Hey, you she-
goats,
stop your skipping or you'll rouse old Billy.

SECOND IDYLL

Where are my bay leaves? Bring them,
Thestylis. And where are the love-charms?
Crown the bowl with fine red wool.
I'll weave a spell against my cruel lover,
who for twelve days now hasn't come near,
the unkind man, and doesn't know
whether I'm alive or dead. Not once
has he knocked at my door, the heartless fellow.
Surely Eros and Aphrodite
have turned his fickle attention elsewhere.
Tomorrow I'm going to Timagetos'
wrestling school to see him, and ask him
why he treats me so badly. But now
I'll put fire-spells on him. Shine brightly,
Selene, for I'll sing softly to you,
goddess, and to Hekate underground,
before whom even the dogs shiver
as she passes over the graves of the dead
and the dark blood. Hail, awful Hekate!
Be my helper to the end.
And make these medicines of mine
as strong as Kirke's or Medeia's
or golden-haired Perimede's.

Magic wheel, draw the man to my house.

First barley grains, to smoulder
on the fire. Sprinkle them, Thestylis.
Idiot! Have you lost your mind?
Must I be made a fool of,
even by you, you sloven?
Sprinkle them on, and say
"I sprinkle the bones of Delphis."

Magic wheel, draw the man to my house.

Delphis has brought me trouble,
and I'm burning this bay against Delphis.

As the bay leaves crackle loudly
and catch fire suddenly
and we don't even see the ashes,
so may Delphis' body burn.

Magic wheel, draw the man to my house.

With help from the goddess, I melt
this wax, and so may Delphis
of Myndos quickly melt with love.
And as this wheel of brass turns,
so, by Aphrodite's power,
may he turn and turn about my door.

Magic wheel, draw the man to my house.

Now I'll burn the husks. O Artemis,
you can move the gates of adamant
in Haides and all other
immovable things. Thestylis,
the dogs howl in the town.
The goddess stands at the crossroads.
Quickly, clash the bronze.

Magic wheel, draw the man to my house.

The sea is still and the wind is still,
but the trouble in my breast
is never still, and I burn
for him who made me a shameful thing—
no wife, but no longer a maiden.

Magic wheel, draw the man to my house.

Three times I pour libation,
and three times, o mistress, I say
whether he lies by a woman
or a man, may he forget them
as Theseus, they say, forgot
blonde Ariadne in Dia.

Magic wheel, draw the man to my house.

An Arkadian weed is horse-madness,
which makes all the colts and swift mares
run in a frenzy on the hills.
May I see Delphis so,
and may he come like a madman
to this house from the oily palaestra.

Magic wheel, draw the man to my house.

Delphis lost this fringe from his cloak.
I pull it to pieces and cast it
into the cruel flames. O bitter Love,
why have you clung like a leech
from the marshes and emptied all
the dark blood from my body?

Magic wheel, draw the man to my house.

I'll grind up a lizard, and tomorrow
I'll bring you an evil drink.
But now, Thestylis, take these ashes
and smear them over his doorposts
while it is night, and whisper
"I smear the bones of Delphis."

Magic wheel, draw the man to my house.

Alone now, how shall I lament
my love? Where shall I begin?
Who brought this evil upon me?
Anaxo, Euboulos' daughter,
came by with a basket for the grove
of Artemis. To honor the goddess
they were parading wild animals
that day, including a lioness.

Mistress Moon, hear how my love began.

And Theumaridas' Thrassan nurse,
who died recently, but lived next door
at the time, begged and implored me
to come and see the show. And I,
unlucky fool, went with her,
wearing a lovely, sweeping dress
of linen, over which I had thrown
Klearista's beautiful cloak.

Mistress Moon, hear how my love began.

And when I had gone halfway
on the road, near Lykon's, I saw
Delphis and Eudamippos walking
together. Their beards were golden
as helichryse and their breasts
brighter far than you, o Selene,
for they had just come from the manly
work of the gymnasium.

Mistress Moon, hear how my love began.

The moment I looked, madness seized me,
and my poor heart was afire.
My good looks faded away. The show
meant nothing to me, and I don't know
how I even got home again.
But a parching fever shook me
and for ten days and ten nights
I lay suffering in my bed.

Mistress Moon, hear how my love began.

And often my skin turned pale
as yellow dye-wood, and my hair
was all falling out, and nothing was left
of me but skin and bones.
To whom didn't I go? What crone's house
didn't I visit, of the ones with skill
in magic? But this was no light thing,
and time went flying by.

Mistress Moon, hear how my love began.

So I told my maid the truth:
"Come, Thestylis, find me some cure
for this wretched disease. The Myndian
possesses me altogether.
Go then, and keep watch for him
by Timagetos' wrestling-school,
for it's there he likes to go and spend his time.

Mistress Moon, hear how my love began.

And when you're sure he's alone,
beckon him secretly and say
'Simaitha wants you to come,'
and bring him here." I said this,
and she went, and brought smooth-skinned Delphis
back to my house. And as soon
as I saw him, light-footed, crossing
the threshold of my door—

Mistress Moon, hear how my love began.

then I turned colder than snow
all over, and sweat broke out
like dewdrops, and I wasn't
able to speak a word, not even
a whimper such as a baby makes
in its sleep, calling its dear mother,

and all my white body became
as stiff as a wax doll.
Mistress Moon, hear how my love began.
And when he had glanced at me,
that false lover, he fixed his eyes
on the ground, and sat on the bed,
and as he sat down, he said
"Believe me, Simaitha, when you called me
to your house, you outran my coming
by no more than I outran
handsome Philinos, the other day.
Mistress Moon, hear how my love began.
For I would have come myself,
by sweet Eros I would, with two
or three friends, once it was night,
carrying apples of Dionysos
in my breast, and on my brow
sprigs of white poplar—the boughs
sacred to Herakles—woven
together with purple bands.
Mistress Moon, hear how my love began.
And if you had let me in,
that would have been a good thing,
for I'm considered good-looking
and athletic among the young men.
And if I'd only kissed your sweet lips,
I'd have slept. But if you had turned me away,
and barred the door, then axes
and torches would have come against you.
Mistress Moon, hear how my love began.
But now I say my thanks are due
first to Kypris, and after her
it's you, young lady, that have caught me
from the burning, when I was almost
consumed, by summoning me
to this dwelling of yours. Often
Eros kindles a hotter blaze
than Hephaistos on Lipara.
Mistress Moon, hear how my love began.
And with his awful frenzy
he drives the maiden from her bedroom

and the bride from her husband's bed
while it's still warm." He said this,
and too easily won, I took him
by the hand and drew him down
on the soft bed. And quickly
body warmed to body, and faces
burned hotter, and we whispered
sweetly. And not to tell you
a long story, dear Selene,
the great thing was accomplished,
and we both came to our desire.

And he found no fault with me
till yesterday, nor I with him.
But today, when the horses were carrying
rosy-armed Dawn from Okean
swiftly up the sky, the mother
of Philista, our flute-player,
and of Melixo came to me.
She told me many other things
and that Delphis was in love.

And she didn't know for certain
whether desire for a woman
or for a man possessed him,
but only this, that his pledge
was always to Eros, in unmixed wine,
and he went away at last in a hurry,
saying he was going to decorate
a certain house with garlands.

These things my visitor told me,
and she's right. For he used to come here
three or four times every day,
and often he'd leave his Dorian
oil-flask with me. But now
it's the twelfth day since I've even
seen him. Mustn't he have found
some other delight, and forgotten me?

Now I'll bind him with my love-charms,
but if he still treats me badly,
by the Fates, he'll do his knocking
on the gates of Haides, I say—
such evil drugs I keep for him
in a box, taught me, o Queen,

by an Assyrian stranger.
But farewell, mistress, and turn
your horses toward Okean. And I
will bear my longing as I've borne it
until now. Farewell, Selene
of the bright throne, and farewell, stars
that follow the wheel of tranquil night.

THIRD IDYLL

I go to sing to Amaryllis
while my she-goats graze on the hill
and Tityros herds them. Tityros,
good friend, feed the she-goats
and lead them to the spring.
But look out for that yellow he-goat,
the Libyan, or he'll butt you.
  O beautiful Amaryllis,
why don't you look out anymore
from your cave, and call me in,
your sweetheart? Do you hate me?
Am I snub-nosed, girl, when seen
close up? Does my beard stick out?
You'll make me hang myself.
Look, I bring you ten apples,
picked where you told me to pick them.
Tomorrow I'll bring you ten more.
Look at me. I'm heartsick.
I wish I were that bumble-bee,
to penetrate those ferns and ivy
where you're hiding, into your cave.
Now I know Eros. He's a cruel god,
suckled on a she-lion's tit,
raised by his mother in the wildwood.
His fire burns me, eating to the bone.
O girl with the lovely glances,
all of stone! Dark-eyebrowed nymph,
come to your goatherd's arms,
so I may kiss you. Even
in empty kisses there's sweet delight.
You'll make me pull to pieces
the ivy wreath I carry,
woven with roses and fragrant parsley,
for you, darling Amaryllis.
What's going to become of me,

poor soul? You won't even listen.
I'll strip off my coat and leap
into the waves from the place
where Olpis, the fisherman,
watches for tunny. If I kill myself,
you, at least, will be happy.
I learned the truth the other day
when I asked myself whether you loved me
and the love-in-absence wouldn't stick
when slapped, but shriveled
uselessly on my smooth forearm.
And Agroio, the sieve-diviner,
when she was gathering herbs,
told me the truth—that my heart
was wholly yours, but that you
cared nothing for me. Listen,
I'm saving you a white she-goat
with two kids which Mermnon's
brown serving-girl begs of me
I'll give it to her, since you won't have me.
Now my right eye's twitching.
Does that mean I'll see her?
I'll lean against this pinetree
and sing. Maybe she'll look out,
if her heart isn't all stone.

Hippomenes, to win the maid,
carried apples in the race.
Atalanta saw, and longed, and plunged
deeply into love.
When the seer Melampos brought from Pylos
home to Othrys the stolen herd,
Alphesiboia's lovely mother
was laid in Bias' arms.
And didn't Adonis, shepherding
his flock upon the hills, inspire
Kythereia to such passion
she embraced his body, dead?
Lucky is Endymion,
sleeping his untroubled sleep,
and lucky Iasion, whose fate,
profane, you'll never know.

My head's aching, but you
don't care. I'll sing no more,
but lie here where I've fallen
and let the wolves eat me.
And may that be as sweet to you
as honey down your throat.

FOURTH IDYLL

Battos.   Tell me, Korydon, whose cows are these? Philondas'?

Korydon.   No, they're Aigon's. He gave them to me to graze

Battos.   And evenings, I suppose, you milk them on the sly?

Korydon.   No, the old man puts the calves to suck, and watches me.

Battos.   And the cowherd himself—where has he disappeared to?

Korydon.   Haven't you heard? Milon took him to the Alpheos.

Battos.   When did he ever set eyes on wrestler's oil?

Korydon.   They say he's like Herakles in strength and toughness.

Battos.   And I'm a better man than Polydeukes, mother says.

Korydon.   He took an exercisingaxe and twenty sheep.

Battos.   Milon will persuade the wolves to go crazy, next.

Korydon.   And the heifers are mooing. They miss their master.

Battos.   The poor beasts. What a sorry cowherd theirs was!

Korydon.   Poor beasts indeed! They don't want to feed anymore.

Battos.   There's nothing left of that calf, over there, but bones.
            Does she live on dewdrops, like a grasshopper?

Korydon.   No, by Zeus. I graze her by the Aisaros
            sometimes, and give her nice handfuls of fresh grass,
            and sometimes she frisks on shady Latymnos.

Battos.   The red bull's thin too. I hope the Lampriadans
            get one like it when the demesmen sacrifice
            to Hera. They're bad neighbors in that deme.

Korydon.   And yet the bull gets driven to the marshes,
            and to Physkos's, and to the Neaithos,
            where all good things grow—goatweed, fleabane,
            and sweet beeplant.

Battos.   Wretched Aigon, your cows will end up in Haides
because you too love a cursed victory.
And the pipe you once made yourself is mildew-
flecked.

Korydon.   No, by the Nymphs, it's not, for since he was going
off to Pisa, he gave it to me. I play a bit
and can strike up Glauke's and Pyrrhos' tunes
rather well.

> I sing the praises of Kroton,
> and Zakynthos is a fine town,
> and the shrine that faces the dawn
> in Lakinion. There Aigon
> the boxer, all by himself,
> devoured eighty loaves, and seized
> the bull by the foot and brought it
> down from the mountain and gave it
> to Amaryllis. And the women
> shrieked loudly and the cowherd laughed.

Battos.   Lovely Amaryllis, we'll never forget you,
even in death. You alone were as dear to me
as my goats, when you died. A bad spirit rules my
fate.

Korydon.   Console yourself, dear Battos. Things may be better
tomorrow. While there's life there's hope. Only
the dead
have none. It's god's will, whether we have sun or
rain.

Battos.   I'll be all right. Drive the calves up from below.
They're eating the olive shoots, the villains!

Korydon.   Out, Whitey,
out, Kymaitha, to the hill. Can't you hear me?
Get out, or by Pan I'll give you a bad end
this minute. Look, there she's creeping back again!
I wish I had my crooked stick. I'd lambaste you!

Battos.   Look here, Korydon! By heaven, a thorn's got me
here under the ankle. How long these spikethorns
are!
Curse that heifer. It pricked me when I was gaping
after her. Do you see it?

Korydon.   Yes, and I've got it
between my nails. There it is.

Battos.   What a tiny
wound, to stop a grown man!

Korydon.   When you go to the hills
don't go barefoot, Battos. Thorns and brambles
     grow
on the hills.

Battos.   Tell me, Korydon, the old man—
is he still after that black-eyebrowed darling
he used to be so crazy about?

Korydon.   More than ever,
poor devil. I came upon them the other day,
myself, by the cowshed, and caught them in the act.

Battos.   Good work, old lecher! You come of the Satyr-kind
and can hold your own with the rough-legged Pans.

FIFTH IDYLL

Komatas. Goats, stay away from that shepherd, Lakon
of Sybaris. He stole my goatskin yesterday.

Lakon. Here, lambs. Away from the spring. Don't you see
that Komatas who stole my pan-pipe recently?

Komatas. What pipe was that? Where did you, Sibyrtas'
slave,
ever get a pipe? And why aren't you satisfied
to play a straw flute anymore, like Korydon?

Lakon. The pipe Lykon gave me, Mister Free. But what
skin
did Lakon ever steal from you? Tell me, Komatas.
Your master, Eumaras, never slept on one.

Komatas. The dappled skin Krokylos gave me, the day
he sacrificed the goat to the Nymphs. And you,
thief,
burned with envy then, and now you've stripped me
naked.

Lakon. By sea-shore Pan, it wasn't Kalaithis' son,
Lakon, who stole your coat. If so, may I go crazy
and leap from this rock into the Krathis below.

Komatas. And by these lake Nymphs, dear sir—may they always
be kind to me, and bring me good fortune—
it wasn't Komatas who stole your pipe.

Lakon. If I believe you, may I suffer troubles
like Daphnis'. But come, if you'll bet a kid—
it's not much—I'll sing with you till you've had
enough.

Komatas. The pig once challenged Athene! But there,
I'll bet the kid. Come, put up a fat lamb.

Lakon. You fox, how would that be fair between us?
Who shears hair for wool, or milks a lousy bitch
instead of a she-goat nursing her first kid?

Komatas. Someone as sure as you of beating his neighbor—
a wasp buzzing against a cicada.
If the kid won't do, here's a he-goat. You go first.

Lakon. What's your hurry? You're not on fire. You'll sing
more pleasantly sitting here among these trees,
under the olive. Cold water trickles here,
and there's grass to sit on, and the locusts chirr.

Komatas. I'm in no hurry, but it vexes me that you
dare to look me in the face—you that I taught
when you were a child. See what kindness comes to!
Raise wolf-cubs, or puppies rather, to devour you.

Lakon. What good thing did I ever learn, or hear
from you, you envious, nasty little fellow?

Komatas. When I made you squeal with pain, and the she-
goats
bleated, and the he-goat leaped upon them.

Lakon. May your grave be no deeper than that thrust,
you hunchback. But come here. Sing your last song.

Komatas. I won't come there. Here are oaks and sedge-grass.
Here the bees hum sweetly about their hives.
Here are two springs of cold water, and the birds
warble in the trees, and the shade's better
than yours, and the pine drops cones from above.

Lakon. Come here, and you'll have lambskins underfoot
and fleeces soft as sleep, while your goatskins
stink worse than you do yourself. And I'll set
a great bowl of white milk for the Nymphs,
and set another of sweet olive-oil.

Komatas. But if you come here, you'll have soft fern
and flowering mint under your feet
and lie on goatskins four times as soft
as your lambskins. And for Pan I'll set
eight bowls of milk and eight of honeycomb.

Lakon. Begin the match from there, then, and sing your
song.
Tread your own ground, and keep your oaks. But
who'll judge?
I wish Lykopas, the cowherd, would come by.

21

Komatas. I can get along without Lykopas.
But if you like, we'll call that fellow Morson,
the woodchopper there, cutting heather near you.

Lakon. Let's call him.

Komatas. Give him a shout.

Lakon.   Hey there, friend,
come here, will you, and listen awhile. We've a bet,
to see who's the better singer. And Morson,
don't favor me, old man, or be too kind to him.

Komatas. Yes, good Morson, by the Nymphs, don't be partial
to Komatas, and don't favor him. This flock
belongs to Sibyrtas of Thourii, friend,
and the goats to Eumaras of Sybaris.

Lakon. By heaven, who asked if the flock was mine
or Sibyrtas', curse you? What a blabbermouth!

Komatas. I tell the whole truth, my fine fellow,
without bragging. It's you that's quarrelsome.

Lakon. Say your say, and let our friend get back to town
alive. By Paian, Komatas, how you babble!

THE SINGING MATCH

Komatas. The Muses love me better than singer Daphnis,
and I offered them two kids the other day.

Lakon. But Apollo loves me dearly. I'm feeding
a fine ram for him. The feast of Karnea's near.

Komatas. The goats I milk have all borne twins, except two.
The girl saw me and said "Too bad you milk alone."

Lakon. Well, well! But Lakon fills almost twenty baskets
with cheese, and lies with a boy among the flowers.

Komatas. Klearista pelts the goatherd with apples
as he drives his goats by, and whistles at him
sweetly.

Lakon. And when gentle Kratidas runs to meet the shepherd,
he maddens me. The bright hair dances on his neck.

Komatas. But briar and anemone can't compare
with rosebeds blossoming by the garden wall.

Lakon. Nor acorns with wild apples. The oak gives acorns
a bitter shell, but apples are honey-sweet.

Komatas. I'll give my girl a ring-dove tomorrow,
taken from the juniper tree where it broods.

Lakon. And when I shear the black ewe, I'll give Kratidas
its soft fleece willingly, to make him a cloak.

Komatas. Here, you bleaters, get away from the olive-trees!
Graze on the hillside, by the tamarisks.

Lakon. Konaros, Kinaitha, come away from that oak!
Graze over here, toward the east, where Phalaros is.

Komatas. I've a pail of cypress-wood, and a mixing-bowl,
Praxiteles' work, that I'm saving for my girl.

Lakon. I've a dog that loves the flock and strangles wolves,
a gift for my boy, to hunt wild beasts of all kinds.

Komatas. You locusts that hop over our fence, take care
not to spoil my vines, for they're young and tender.

Lakon. You cicadas, see how I provoke the goatherd.
Just so, I think, do you provoke the reapers.

Komatas. I hate the foxes with their bushy tails that come
every evening to steal grapes from Mikon's vineyard.

Lakon. And I hate the beetles, borne upon the wind,
that come to nibble at Philondas' figs.

Komatas. Don't you remember how I let you have it,
and you grinned and wriggled, clinging to that oak?

Lakon. That I don't remember, but I know very well
how Eumaras once bound you there and beat you.

Komatas. See, Morson, somebody's losing his temper now.
Go quickly, pick lilies from some old woman's grave.

Lakon. And I'm stinging someone too, as you can see,
Morson. Go to the Haleis and dig cyclamen.

Komatas. Let Himera flow with milk instead of water,
and Krathis red with wine, and its reeds bear fruit.

Lakon. Let Sybaris flow with honey, and at dawn
the girl dip honey, not water, in her pail.

Komatas. My goats feed on clover and goatweed, and walk
on mastic, and take their rest on arbutus.

Lakon. My sheep have bee-plant to browse on, and cistus
flourishes in plenty everywhere, like roses.

23

Komatas.   I don't love Alkippe, for she wouldn't kiss me,
             holding me by the ears, when I gave her the dove.

Lakon.   But I love Eumedes dearly. When I gave him
             the shepherd's pipe he kissed me very sweetly.

Komatas.   Jays shouldn't contend with nightingales, Lakon,
             or hoopoes with swans. But you, fool, love to
               quarrel.

Morson.   I bid the shepherd cease, and to you, Komatas,
             Morson awards the lamb. When you sacrifice it
             to the Nymphs, send a good piece quickly to
               Morson.

Komatas.   I'll send it, by Pan. Now, all my flock of goats,
             snort for joy. See what a good laugh I'll have
             against Lakon the shepherd, for I've won the lamb
             at last. I'll leap sky-high for you. Be merry,
             my horned goats. I'll take you all tomorrow
             for a dip in Sybaris pond. You there,
             you white billy-goat, I'll geld you if you dare
             mount one of my shes, before I've sacrificed
             the lamb to the Nymphs. There he goes again!
             If I don't castrate you, let them call me
             Melanthios instead of Komatas.

SIXTH IDYLL

Damoitas and Daphnis the cowherd
once gathered their herds together
in one place, Aratos. The chin
of one was golden with down,
the other's beard was half grown.
And beside a spring they sat down
together in the summer noon
and sang. And Daphnis began,
for he first proposed the match:

Galateia is pelting your flock
with apples, Polyphemos,
and calls you a backward lover
and a goatherding fellow.
And you, silly fool, won't even
glance at her, but sit there
piping sweetly away. Look,
now she's throwing them at the dog
that follows you and helps watch
your sheep, and it looks in the water
and barks, and the bright waves
that splash gently mirror it
as it runs along the shore.
Take care that it doesn't spring
at her legs when she comes from the sea
and injure her lovely skin.
See how she stands there flirting,
and as lightly as dry thistledown
in fine summer weather, flies
from the lover, but when he loves not,
pursues, and leaves no trick untried.
Often, Polyphemos, what is not
seems beautiful to love.

After him, Damoitas played
a prelude, and began to sing:

By Pan, I saw her pelting
my flock. She didn't escape me
nor my one sweet eye, with which
I'll go on seeing to the end.
Let Telemos the soothsayer
carry home his evil prophecies
and keep them for his children.
It's to tease her I won't look back,
and say I love another girl.
And when she hears that, she's jealous
of me, by Paian. And she pines,
and looks from the sea in a frenzy
at my caves and my flock.
I set the dog to bark at her,
for when I was courting her,
he'd nuzzle her legs and whine.
Perhaps when she sees me doing this
a few times, she'll send a messenger.
But I'll bar the door till she swears
to make me with her own hands
a fine bed on this island.
For I'm really not so ugly
as they say. A while ago,
I was looking into the sea
when it was calm, and my beard
was beautiful, it seemed to me,
and my one eye looked beautiful.
And my teeth, reflected in the sea,
gleamed whiter than Parian stone.
But to ward off an evil fate,
I spat three times in my breast,
as old Kotyttaris taught me.

Then Damoitas kissed Daphnis,
after he had sung, and gave him
a pipe, and the other gave him
a lovely flute. And Damoitas
began to flute, and Daphnis,
the cowherd, to pipe, and soon
the calves were skipping in the soft grass.
Neither won the victory,
for they both were unbeatable.

SEVENTH IDYLL

Once Eukritos and I set out
from town for the Haleis, and Amyntas
made it three. A harvest feast
for Demeter was being given
by Phrasidamos and Antigenes,
the two sons of Lykopeos,
famous for his noble birth,
being descended from Klytia
and Chalkon himself, who struck
his hard knee against the rock
and brought Bourina fountain
gushing at his feet. Nearby,
elms and poplars wove green arches
overhead to make a shady place.
But before we had gone halfway
or come in sight of Brasilas' tomb,
by the Muses' grace we overtook
a fine fellow from Kydonia
named Lykidas. He was a goatherd,
as anyone could tell, for he looked
exactly like one. He wore
a rough brown goatskin on his shoulder,
still smelling of rennet, and across
his chest a broad belt strapped in
an old tunic. In his right hand
he carried a crooked olive stick.
He smiled quietly, and with mocking eyes
he spoke to me, a grin still hanging
on his lip. "Well, Simichidas,
where are you rushing to, at noon,
when even the lizard sleeps in the wall,
and the crested larks desert the fields?
Are you invited to some banquet,
or is it a townsman's wine-party
that makes you hurry so? You're going

so fast your shoes send the pebbles
spinning and ringing." I answered
"Lykidas, my friend, they tell me
you're the best of the herdsmen and reapers
at piping. I'm glad to hear it.
But I think I'm as good as you.
We're on our way to a harvest feast
where some friends are offering first-fruits
from their store to fine-robed Demeter.
For the goddess has piled their threshing-floor
with abundance of fat barley.

But come, since the day and the way
bring us together, let us sing
country songs, and perhaps we can learn
something from each other. For I, too,
speak with the Muses' clear voice,
and I'm called an excellent singer,
though I don't believe everything
I hear, by Zeus. For I know
I can't match the great Sikelidas
of Samos in singing, yet,
or Philitas, but vie with them
like a bullfrog with cicadas."

I said this deliberately,
and the goatherd laughed and said
"Here's my stick, for you're a sapling
Zeus has fashioned from the true stock.
How I hate the stonemason who tries
to build his house up as high
as the top of Mount Oromedon.

And I hate those cocks of the Muses
who challenge the Chian nightingale
with their foolish crowing. But come,
let's begin our pastoral song
at once, Simichidas, and I—
but friend, see how it strikes you,
this song I made one day on the hill.

Ageanax will have good sailing
to Mitylene when the Kids
stand in the western sky, and waves
scud before the south wind, and Orion
sets his foot upon Okean,

if he'll rescue Lykidas,
scorched in Aphrodite's fire,
for I burn with love for him.
And halcyons will calm the waves
and the sea, the south wind and the east,
which churns the seaweed to the bottom—
halcyons whom beyond all birds
the green Nereids love, and those
who make their living from the sea.
Ageanax is sailing to Mitylene:
may the season favor him
and fair winds blow him to port.
And on that day I'll bind my head
with dill and snowdrops and roses,
and drink Ptelean wine from a cup,
and lie by the fire. And I'll roast
beans on the fire. And my bed
will be piled to the elbow with fleabane
and asphodel and crinkled parsley.
Thinking of Ageanax, I'll drink,
and drain the cup to the bottom.
And two shepherds will pipe to me—
one from Acharnae and one from Lykope.
And beside me Tityros will sing
how cowherd Daphnis loved Xenea,
and the hills took pity on him,
and the oaks on Himeras' banks
sang dirges because he was wasting
with love like the snows on Haimos
or on Athos or Rhodope
or the distant Kaukasos.
And how once a wicked king
prisoned a goatherd alive
in a great chest, and snub-nosed bees
came to the sweet-smelling cedar box
from the fields and fed him on flowers
because his mouth had been filled
with nectar by the Muses.
Such was your fate, blessed Komatas—
shut up in a chest, fed on honey,
you lived through the spring of the year.
I wish you had lived in my day.

I'd graze your fine goats on the hill
and listen to your voice while you lay
beneath the oaks or the pinetrees
and sang to me, godlike Komatas."

He sang this much and stopped. And I said
"Lykidas, the Nymphs have taught me
many good things, my friend, while I grazed
my flocks on the hills, and their fame
may have reached to Zeus's throne.
But the best of them all by far
is this one I'll sing for your pleasure.
Listen, for the Muses love you:

The loves sneezed for Simichidas,
for the poor man loves his girl Myrto
the way goats love the spring.
But my best friend, Aratos,
is secretly in love with a boy.

Aristis, a good man—one
of the very best, whom Phoibos
himself would permit to sing
beside his tripods with his lyre—
he knows how love for the boy
burns Aratos to the bone.

You, Pan, master of Homole's
beautiful plain, put the boy
unbidden in my dear friend's arms,
whether it is gentle Philinos
or another. If you do, dear Pan,
may the boys of Arkadia
never beat you over the shoulders
and thighs with squills when their meat
is scarce. But if you won't,
may you be bitten all over,
and scratch yourself with your nails,
and sleep on nettles, and in winter
live in the Edonian hills
facing Hebros river near the Bear.

And in summer may your herding be
in far-off Aithiopia,
beside the Blemyan Rock,
beyond which Neilos can't be seen

anymore. But you, Loves,
rosy as apples, leave Hyetis
and the sweet river of Byblis
and steep Oikos, golden-haired
Dione's home, and shoot with your bows
handsome Philinos. Shoot him,
for the silly boy has no pity
for my friend. And yet he's overripe,
like a pear, and the women cry,
'Poor Philinos, your bloom's fading fast.'
Come, Aratos, let's watch no more
at his door, and wear our feet out.
Let the crowing cock deliver
someone else to the numbing chill
of morning. Friend, let Molon
suffer by himself in that school.
But let our minds seek quietness
while we keep an old crone handy
to spit on us and keep evil away."
This I sang, and Lykidas laughed
again pleasantly, and gave me his stick
in fellowship of the Muses,
and turned left, taking the road
to Pyxa, but Eukritos
and handsome Amyntas and I
turned off at Phrasidamos's
and happily laid ourselves down
on beds of sweet grass and vine-leaves,
freshly picked. Overhead, many elms
and poplars rustled, and nearby
the sacred waters splashed down
from the Nymphs' cave. Brown cicadas
shrilled from the shady branches,
and far off the tree-frog whined
in the heavy underbrush.
Larks and finches sang, doves crooned,
and bees hummed about the spring.
Everything smelled of rich summer
and rich fruits. Pears lay at our feet,
apples in plenty rolled beside us,
and branches loaded down with plums
bent to the ground. And we broke

the four-year seals on the wine-jars.
Nymphs of Kastalia that live
on the slopes of Parnassos, tell me,
was it such a cup old Chiron
offered Herakles in Pholos'
rocky cave? Was it a drink like this
set Polyphemos dancing,
that mighty shepherd who grazed
his flocks beside the Anapos
and pelted ships with mountains—
such nectar as you mixed for us,
you Nymphs, that day by the altar
of Demeter of the Harvest?
May I plant the great winnowing-fan
another time in her grain-heaps,
while she stands and smiles at us
with wheat-sheaves and poppies in her hands.

EIGHTH IDYLL

Herding his sheep on the high hills,
Menalkas met handsome Daphnis,
pasturing his cattle there.
Both were auburn-haired, both young,
both skillful in piping and singing.
Seeing Daphnis, Menalkas began:
"Daphnis, herder of mooing cows,
will you sing against me?
I say I can outsing you,
if the songs are as long as I choose."
Daphnis answered "Piper Manalkas,
keeper of woolly sheep, you'll never
beat me, even if you sing
till you injure yourself."

Menalkas. Will you prove it, then? Will you bet?

Daphnis. I'll prove it. And I'll make a bet.

Menalkas. What will we bet, then, against what?

Daphnis. I'll bet a calf and you a lamb
as big as its mother.

Menalkas.   Never
will I bet a lamb, for my father
is strict, and so is my mother,
and they count the sheep at night.

Daphnis. Then what will you bet? What's the winner
to get?

Menalkas.   A lovely pan-pipe
of nine reeds, fitted smoothly,
top and bottom, with white wax.
I made it myself. I'll bet that,
but not what belongs to my father.

Daphnis. I too have a pipe of nine reeds,
fitted smoothly with white wax,
top and bottom. I made it

the other day, and this finger's
still sore where a split reed cut me.

Menalkas. But who'll listen to us and judge?

Daphnis. Let's call that goatherd over there—
the one whose white-spotted dog
is barking around the kids.
The boys shouted, and the goatherd
heard them and came. The boys got ready
to sing and the goatherd to judge them.
First, clear-voiced Menalkas sang,
for the lot had fallen to him,
and Daphnis sang the answering part
in country song. Menalkas began:

Menalkas. Valleys and rivers, born of the gods,
if ever piper Menalkas pleased you
with a song, feed his lambs willingly,
and if Daphnis ever brings his calves,
let him be granted no less.

Daphnis. Meadows and wells, sweet pasturage,
if Daphnis sings like the nightingales,
fatten his herd. And if Menalkas
drives his flocks here, let him find
welcome, and excellent grazing.

Menalkas. There the sheep and goats bear twins,
and bees fill the hives with honey,
and the oaks grow taller, wherever
handsome Milon walks. If he goes,
shepherd and pasture wither.

Daphnis. Everywhere it's spring, and pastures
are everywhere, and udders
swell with milk, and the yearlings suck,
wherever beautiful Nais wanders.
If she goes, cows and cowherd are wasted.

Menalkas. You he-goat, mate of the white she-goats,
into the forest's great depths
(stay here, you blunt-nosed kids, by the spring)
for he is there. Go, stump-horn, and say
"Milon, Proteus herded seals, though a god."

Daphnis. [*Daphnis' reply is missing.*]

Menalkas. I don't want Pelops' land, or Kroisos'
money, nor to outrun the winds.

But I'll sit under this rock and sing
with you in my arms, watching
my flocks grazing, and the Sikelian sea.

Daphnis.   The tempest is ruinous to trees,
drought to waters, snares to birds,
nets to game. But to man, desire
for a tender girl. Father Zeus,
not I alone am lovesick.
You loved women too.

Thus the boys sang back and forth,
and Menalkas led the last song:

Menalkas.   Wolf, spare my kids and mother-goats,
and don't harm me, for I'm young
to look after so large a flock.
Lampouros, my dog, are you sleeping
so soundly? Heavy sleeping's
not for a dog that herds with a boy.

My ewes, eat the tender grass freely.
It will grow again before
you're tired of it. Feed all,
fill your udders, so the lambs
will have enough, and the rest
I'll store in cheesebaskets.

Then Daphnis followed, with clear-voiced song:

Daphnis.   Yesterday, from her cave,
a girl with meeting eyebrows
spied me driving my heifers by.
And she cried "How handsome he is—
how handsome!" But I
didn't even answer her back,
but looked down and kept on my way.

    The heifer's voice is sweet,
and her breath is sweet, and sweet
to lie by a running stream
under the sky in summer.
Acorns, pride of the oak,
apples, of the apple tree,
calf, of the cow, and cows
the only pride of the cowherd.

Thus the boys sang, and the goatherd
said "Daphnis, your mouth is sweet,

and your voice is beautiful.
I'd rather listen to your songs
than eat honey. Take the pipes,
for you're the winner in singing.

If you'll teach me to sing too
as I herd my goats beside you,
I'll pay you for your teaching
with this stump-horned goat that always
fills the milk-pail over the brim."

The boy was delighted with winning,
and clapped his hands, and leaped
for joy, the way a fawn leaps
around its dam. But the other
smouldered, sick at heart
with grief, the way a young girl
will grieve on her wedding-day.

And Daphnis was first of the herdsmen
from that day, and while still a young man
he married the nymph Nais.

NINTH IDYLL

Sing a pastoral song, Daphnis,
and begin the singing. You first,
Daphnis, and you, Menalkas,
follow when you've put the calves
beneath the cows, and the bulls
with the barren heifers, to graze
together and wander in the grove
but never stray from the herd.
Sing to me from your side,
and Menalkas answer from the other.

Daphnis.   Sweetly sounds the calf, and the cow,
and sweetly the cowherd with his pipe,
and sweetly I. Beside the cool brook
is my bed of leaves piled with fine skins
of white calves the evil southwest wind
swept from the cliff as they browsed
on arbutus. And I care
no more for scorching summer
than a lover cares for the words
of his father or his mother.

Thus Daphnis sang. And Menalkas:

Menalkas.   Aitna, my mother, I too
have a fine cave to live in
among the hollow rocks, and there
I've everything we behold
in dreams—many ewes and she-goats,
and their fleeces lying at my head
and my feet. And on my fire
of oak-logs, puddings are baking,
and dry chestnuts are roasting there
when it's winter. And I care
no more for winter than a man
who's toothless cares for walnuts
when soft cakes are handy.

Then I clapped my hands and gave them
each a gift right away: to Daphnis
a staff that grew on my father's farm,
self-shaped, yet even a craftsman
might have found no fault with it;
to the other a lovely conch-shell
I found on the Ikarian rocks,
and ate its meat, after cutting
five shares for the five of us.
And he blew a blast on the shell.
Farewell, pastoral Muses.
Make known the song I sang
that day with the herdsmen. And never
let pimples grow on my tongue-tip.

    Cicada is dear to cicada,
ant to ant, hawk to hawk,
but to me the Muses and song.
With song let my house be full,
for sleep is not more sweet,
or the sudden coming of spring,
or flowers to the honeybees,
so dear to me are the Muses.
For those they look on with favor
Kirke cannot harm with her spells.

TENTH IDYLL

Milon.	What's the matter, farmer Boukaios, poor fellow?
	You can't cut a straight swath anymore, or keep up
	with your reaping-partner. You're lagging, the way a ewe
	lags behind the flock, when her foot's pricked with a thorn.
	What'll you be like at evening, or afternoon,
	if now at the start you can't bite into the row?
Boukaios.	Lateworking Milon, you chip of stubborn granite,
	haven't you ever longed for someone that's absent?
Milon.	Never! A working man shouldn't think beyond his work.
Boukaios.	But haven't you ever lain awake for love?
Milon.	God forbid! A dog shouldn't learn to like pudding.
Boukaios.	But I've been in love for nearly ten days, Milon.
Milon.	You draw from the wine-cask. Vinegar's scarce with me.
Boukaios.	And my dooryard garden's gone unhoed since the planting.
Milon.	What girl's got you going?
Boukaios.	Polybotas' girl,
	who piped to the reapers last week at Hippokion's.
Milon.	God finds out the guilty. You've been asking for it.
	You'll have a grasshopper to cuddle you all night.
Boukaios.	You're making fun of me now. But Ploutos isn't
	the only blind god. There's Eros. So don't talk big.
Milon.	I'm not talking big. Just reap the grain, and strike up
	a love-song for the girl. You'll work more happily
	that way. You were a singer in the old days.
Boukaios sings:	Pierian Muses, sing with me

of the slender girl, for your touch,
goddesses, turns all things lovely.
Charming Bombyka, they call you
Syrian, skinny, and sunburnt,
but I call you honey-skinned.
Dark is the violet, and dark
the monogrammed iris. But these
are chosen first for the garlands.
The goat runs after clover,
wolf chases goat, and the crane
follows the plow. I long for you.
If I had the wealth of Kroisos,
we'd stand there, both, in gold,
offerings to Aphrodite—
you with your pipes, or a rose
or an apple, and I in robes
and fine new Amyklaian shoes.
Charming Bombyka, your feet
are knucklebones, your voice
a poppy, your ways past telling.

Milon. We never knew Boukaios could make such fine
songs.
How well he measured and shaped his melody!
So little good it's done me to grow a beard!
But hear too these lines of godlike Lityerses:

Demeter, rich in fruit and grain,
let our crop be easily reaped
and fruitful beyond expectation.
Bind the sheaves, binders, or they'll say
as they pass "These are figwood men.
Their wages are money wasted."
Let the cut end of your sheaf
face the northwind, or the west.
That way the grain will be fattest.
When you thresh the grain, don't sleep
at noon, for at noon the chaff
parts easiest from the stalk.
But begin your reaping with the lark
and stop when he goes to bed,
but rest in the heat of the day.

The frog's is a happy life, boys.
He needs no one to pour his drink,
for he has it by him in plenty.
Boil us better lentils, steward,
you miser, or you'll cut your hand
when you're splitting cummin-seed.

That's the song for men who work in the sun
to sing.
But as for your starveling love, Boukaios—tell it
to your mother when she wakes in bed in the
morning.

ELEVENTH IDYLL

There's no remedy for love, Nikias,
no unguent, no salve—
except the Muses. That's a gentle
medicine, and pleasant for mortals,
but hard to find—as you know well,
being a physician and favored
by all the nine. In this way
my countryman, Old Polyphemos
the Kyklops consoled himself,
when with still downy cheeks and lips
he loved Galateia. He loved
not with apples, or roses,
or locks of hair, but with a frenzy,
counting everything else but trifles.
Often his sheep came back untended
from the green meadows to the fold,
while he pined away with love,
alone by the wrack-littered shore,
and sang of Galateia all day long,
stung to the heart by the great Kyprian
goddess' shaft. Yet he found the remedy,
and sitting on a peak of rock,
he gazed at the sea and sang:
    O white Galateia—whiter
than curds, softer than lambs,
more wanton than calves, and smoother-
skinned than the unripened grape—
why deny your lover? How is it,
when sweet sleep comes over me,
you're here, and when sweet sleep leaves me,
you're gone—flying like the ewe
when she spies the gray wolf?
I fell in love with you, girl,
when you first came with my mother
to pick hyacinths on the hill,

and I showed you the way.
And seeing you once, from then to now
I've never stopped. But you don't care.
You don't care at all.
I know, sweet girl, why you fly.
It's this shaggy eyebrow, stretching
across my forehead—one long
unbroken brow from ear to ear—
and the one eye beneath, and the broad
nostril above my lip. Such am I,
but I tend a thousand sheep,
and get from them the best milk
to drink. And I've plenty of cheeses.
Summer, fall, middle of winter,
my cheese-baskets are full.
And I can outpipe all other
Kyklops here, as often at night
I sing of you and me,
my apple-sweet darling. I raise
eleven fawns, white-collared,
and four bear-cubs, just for you.

Come to me, then, and you'll lack
nothing. Leave the gray sea
to beat against the shore. You'll pass
the night more pleasantly with me
in my cave. There are baytrees
and slim cypresses nearby,
and dark ivy, and sweet grapes
in bunches, and cold water
that tree-covered Aitna sends
trickling down to me from her snows—
a drink for gods. Who, before these,
would choose the sea and the waves?

But if it's my rough looks
that put you off, I've oak-logs
and banked fires, under the ashes,
and I'd let you burn my soul out,
or my one eye, most dear to me
of all things that are mine.
If only my mother had borne me
with gills, I'd dive down there

43

and kiss your hand, if you wouldn't
let me kiss your mouth. And bring you
snowdrops or soft poppies
with red petals. But one grows
in summer, the other in winter,
so I couldn't bring both together.
Even now, my girl, I'll learn to swim
if some stranger sails this way
in his ship, so I'll know
why it is you choose to live in the sea.
Come forth, Galateia, and forget
as you come—as I do, sitting here—
to go home again. Choose, rather,
shepherding with me, and milking,
and setting cheeses with sour rennet.
It's my mother alone who wrongs me,
and her I blame. Never once
has she spoken a kind word for me
to you, though she sees me growing
thinner every day. I'll tell her
my head aches, and both my feet.
Since I suffer, let her suffer too.
O Kyklops, Kyklops, where
have your wits gone wandering?
You'd show more sense to go weaving
cheesebaskets, or gathering green limbs
for your lambs. Milk the ewe
that's handy. Why pursue
the one that runs away? You'll find,
perhaps, another and fairer
Galateia. Many a girl
teases me to play with her
all night long, and they giggle
when I listen to them. On land,
it seems I'm a somebody too.

Thus Polyphemos shepherded
his love with singing, and found relief
better than if he had spent money.

TWELFTH IDYLL

You have come, dear boy. With the third
night and morning, you have come.
But longing men grow old in a day.
As spring is sweeter than winter,
apple than sloe; as the ewe
has a thicker fleece than her lamb,
and a young maiden surpasses
a thrice-married wife; as the fawn
is swifter-footed than the calf,
and the clear-voiced nightingale
sings best of all winged things;
so your coming has made me glad.
And the way a traveler hurries
to the shady oak when the sun
is scorching, I hurry to you.
May the Loves breathe on us both
equally, till we become
a song for all later men:
"These two were excellent friends
among people of the old days—
one the Inspirer, as they say
among the Amyklaians,
the other called the Hearer
in the speech of Thessalia.
An equal yoke of friendship
they bore. There were men of gold then,
when the loved one returned his love."
Father Zeus, and you unaging
immortals, grant this, and then,
in two hundred generations
let someone bring me this word
beside Acheron, from which none return:
"Your love and your charming Hearer's
still live in all men's mouths,
but the young men's most of all."

The heavenly gods determine
these things. It will be as they choose.
But when I praise your kindness,
no pimples will grow on my nose,
for if you hurt me sometimes,
you heal the pain right away,
and give me a double joy.
With overmeasure I come home.

Megarians of Nisaia,
you champions of the oar,
live happily, for you above all
honored the Attik stranger,
Diokles, lover of his friend.

And each year in early spring
boys gather around his tomb
and contend for the kissing-prize.

And whoever most sweetly touches
lip to lip, goes home to his mother
crowned with garlands. Happy is he
who judges the kisses for the boys,
and earnestly he must pray
to bright Ganymedes that his lips
will be like the Lydian stone
where the money-changers try gold
to see if it is false or true.

THIRTEENTH IDYLL

Not for us alone, Nikias,
as we used to think, was Eros
begotten, whoever of the gods
was his father. We aren't the first
to whom beauty seems beautiful,
who are mortal and can't foresee
the morrow. Even Amphitryon's
bronze-hearted son, who withstood
the savage lion, loved a boy—
charming Hylas, whose hair hung down
in curls. And like a father
with his dear son, he taught him all the things
which had made him a mighty man
and famous. And he never left him,
either at high noon, or when Dawn
races upward with her white horses
to Zeus's house, or when peeping chicks
scurry toward their nest, while the mother
perches on the smoke-stained beam
and flaps her wings. That way the boy
might grow the way he wanted him to,
and yoked with him, attain
the true measure of a man.
And when Iason, Aison's son,
sailed after the golden fleece,
and all the noblest went with him,
chosen from all the cities,
to rich Iolkos he came too,
the man of many labors,
son of noble Alkmena,
queen of Midea. And Hylas
went with him aboard the Argo,
the strong-thwarted ship which never
touched the dark-blue clashing-rocks,
but darted through them and sped

like an eagle over the sea
to the deep Phasis' great gulf.
And the rocks stand fixed from that day.
And when the Pleiades rise,
and the young lambs are pastured
in upland fields, and spring begins
to wane, then that godlike band
of heroes turned their thoughts
to seafaring, and sitting down
to their oars in the hollow Argo,
reached Hellespontos after three days
of wind from the south, and anchored
in the Propontis, where the oxen
of the Kianians, plowing
broad furrows, wear the plowshares bright.

They went ashore, and two by two
made ready their evening meal,
but they made one sleeping-place
for all, where they found a meadow
plentiful with litter for their beds,
and cut sharp rushes and thick sedge-grass.
And golden-haired Hylas had gone
with a bronze pitcher to bring water
for Herakles and brave Telemon,
since the two friends always took supper
together. And soon, in a hollow,
he spied a spring where thick rushes,
and dark celandine, and green
maidenhair, and sweet parsley,
and creeping deergrass grew.
In the water, Nymphs were preparing
for the dance—the sleepless Nymphs,
goddesses feared by country folk,
Eunika, Malis, and Nycheia
with eyes like spring. And as the boy
reached down with the great pitcher,
eager to dip it in the well,
they all clung to his hand, for love
of the Argive boy had fluttered
all their tender hearts. And down
into the dark pool he fell
headlong, the way a flaming star

falls headlong into the sea
from the sky, and a sailor
cries out to his mates "Make fast
the sails, lads, for the wind freshens."
Then the Nymphs held the weeping boy
on their knees, to comfort him
with kind words, but Amphitryon's son
was troubled about the boy
and went out, carrying his bow,
bent in the Maiotian fashion,
and the club he always held
in his right hand. "Hylas!" he called
three times, as loud as he could
with his deep voice, and the boy
answered three times, but his voice
came faintly through the water,
and though near, he seemed far away.
When a savage lion hears
a fawn crying in the mountains
far away, he hurries from his lair
to seize the waiting meal.
And so Herakles went raging
through trackless briars, longing
for the boy, and ranged over much country.
Lovers are reckless. How he toiled
through hills and thickets as he wandered,
Iason's quest completely forgotten.
The Argo lay ready, sails hoisted,
with all the others on board,
but again at midnight the heroes
lowered sail, waiting for Herakles,
while he wandered madly, wherever
his footsteps led him. A cruel god
was rending the heart within him.
Thus loveliest Hylas is numbered
among the blest, but the heroes
mocked Herakles for a runaway
because he deserted the Argo
of the thirty thwarts and came
on foot to the land of Kolchis
and inhospitable Phasis.

FOURTEENTH IDYLL

Aischines.   Greetings, master Thyonichos.

Thyonichos.   The same to you, Aischines.
It's been a long time.

Aischines.   A long time
indeed.

Thyonichos.   What's on your mind?

Aischines.   Things haven't been going well
with me, Thyonichos.

Thyonichos.   That's why
you're so thin, then, and wear
all that stubble on your lip
and this long hair, uncombed.
A Pythagorist showed up,
the other day, looking just so—
barefoot and pale. He called himself
an Athenian.

Aischines.   Then he
was in love too?

Thyonichos.   I think so—
with wheaten bread.

Aischines.   You always
have your joke, my friend. As for me,
beautiful Kyniska scorns me.
I'll go out of my mind, some day,
when nobody expects it.
I'm on the verge now.

Thyonichos.   You're always
this way, Aischines—a bit flighty,
and wanting everything your own way.
But tell me, what's the matter now?

Aischines.   The Argive and I, and that Thessalian
horse-trainer, Agis, and Kleunikos
the mercenary, were drinking together

at my farm. I'd killed two chickens
and a sucking pig, and opened
some Bibline wine—four years old,
almost, and still as fragrant
as the day it was pressed.
And I'd got out some onions and snails.
It was a fine drinking party.
And when everything was going along
nicely, we decided each of us
would drink a toast in unmixed wine
to anyone he chose, but must tell
who it was. And while we drank
and called out names as agreed,
she said nothing, though I was there.
How do you think I liked that?
"Can't you speak? Have you seen a wolf?"
somebody said, for a joke. "Clever,
aren't you?" she said, and blushed.
You could have lighted a candle,
easily, from her face.
There's a Wolf—his *name's* Wolf—
our neighbor Labes' son,
tall and smooth-skinned—many
consider him good-looking.
That fine passion that burned in her
was for him. It had reached my ears
one day, secretly, but I never
looked into it, so little good
it's done me to grow a beard.
Well, the four of us were already
pretty drunk, and that fellow
from Larisa sang "My Wolf"
all the way through—it's some
Thessalian song, the trouble-maker.
And Kyniska suddenly began
to cry, worse than a six-year-old
crying for her mother's lap.
Then I—you know me, Thyonichos—
hit her one with my fist
on the cheek, and then another.
She caught up her skirts and went
as fast as she could go.

"Slut!" I said. "So I'm not good enough
for you? You like some other sweetheart
better? Well, go cuddle up
to your other friend. Weep tears
as big as apples for him."
Quicker than the swallow
that brings a morsel to her babies
under the eaves and is off again
for a fresh one, Kyniska flew
from her soft chair through the hall
and out the door, wherever
her feet carried her. "The bull
took to the woods," as the saying goes.
Twenty. Then eight, then nine,
and another ten. Today's
the eleventh. Add two, and it makes
two months we've been apart,
and if I'm barbered Thrakian-style,
she doesn't know it. Now,
Wolf's everything to her,
and it's for him her door's open
every night, and I don't count—
out of the reckoning altogether,
like the wretched Megarians,
in the lowest place of all.

If only I could get over caring,
everything would be all right.
But now, how can I? I'm like
the mouse that tasted pitch,
as they say, Thyonichos,
and what the remedy is
for hopeless love, I don't know.
Except that Simos, who loved
that brassy girl, went abroad
and came back cured—a man
my own age. I'll cross the sea, too.
A soldier isn't the worst,
or the best, perhaps, but as good
as another.

Thyonichos.   I wish everything
had worked out the way you wanted it,

Aischines, but if you really
mean to expatriate yourself,
Ptolemaios is the best paymaster
for a free man.

Aischines.   What's he like
in other ways?

Thyonichos.   The best.
Gentle, a lover of the arts,
and of women. A good companion.
Knows his friends, and his enemies
even better. He's generous
to many, as a king
should be, and never refuses
anyone—but you musn't
be always asking, Aischines.
So if you decide to pin up
the top corner of your cloak
to your right shoulder, and can stand
firm on your two feet against
a strong man's charge, off you go
to Aigyptos. We're all turning gray
downward from the temples, and time
is whitening our cheeks, hair by hair.
We ought to be doing things
while our knee-joints are still supple.

FIFTEENTH IDYLL

Gorgo.   Is Praxinoa at home?

Praxinoa.   Gorgo!
Of course I'm at home! Darling,
how long it's been. It's a wonder
you got here at all. Eunoa,
get her a chair. And put
a cushion on it.

Gorgo.   It will do
very well as it is.

Praxinoa.   Do sit down, then.

Gorgo.   I'm a helpless thing, Praxinoa.
I barely got here alive
through all the crowds and chariots—
big boots and men in soldiers' cloaks
all over the place, and the road
going on forever. You really
live too far out.

Praxinoa.   It's that crazy
husband of mine. He comes
out here to the ends of the earth
and buys a shed, not a house,
just so we won't be neighbors—
out of sheer spite, the brute!
He's always the same.

Gorgo.   Darling,
don't talk about your man, Dinon,
like that when the little one's around.
See, woman, how he's staring at you.
There, there, Zopyrion, honey.
She doesn't mean Daddy.

Praxinoa.   Heavens!
The child understands.

Gorgo.   Nice Daddy!

Praxinoa.	All the same, that daddy, the other day—
	it was just the other day I told him,
	"Dad, go get some soda and rouge
	at the streetstall," and he came back
	with salt, the big lummox.
Gorgo.	Mine's the same. Money's nothing
	to Diokleides. Just yesterday
	for seven drachmas he bought
	dog's hair, pluckings of old wallets—
	five fleeces, he called them—
	nothing but trash, and work
	on top of work. But come,
	get on your dress and cloak.
	Let's go and see the Adonis
	at the King's, wealthy Ptolemaios'.
	I hear the Queen's got up a fine show.
Praxinoa.	Everything's fine in fine houses.
Gorgo.	What you've seen, you can talk about,
	when *you've* seen it, and others haven't.
	It's time to go.
Praxinoa.	Every day's a day off
	for people with nothing to do.
	Eunoa, you sloven, pick up the spinning.
	Cats love soft sleeping. Hurry,
	bring me some water, quickly.
	Water I ask for, first, and she brings me soap!
	Well, give it here. Not so much,
	you spendthrift! Now the water.
	Idiot, you're soaking my robe!
	That'll do. I've washed as well
	as heaven will let me. Now where's
	the key to the big chest?
	Bring it here.
Gorgo.	Praxinoa!
	That full skirt suits you perfectly.
	Tell me, how much was it,
	just off the loom?
Praxinoa.	Don't remind me,
	Gorgo. More than two minas,
	hard cash, and I worked
	my heart out over it.

Gorgo.   Anyway,
you can tell yourself it's worth it.

Praxinoa.   Fetch my cloak and hood and adjust them
properly. No, I won't take you,
baby. Bad horsey! Bites!
Go ahead and cry. I can't have you
crippled for life. Phrygia,
take baby and play with him.
Call in the dog. And lock the front door.

Heavens, what a crowd!
How will we ever get through the mob?
They're like ants. You can't even count them.

You've done many good things for us,
Ptolemaios, since your father
joined the immortals. Nowadays
no ruffian slips up on you
in the street, Aigyptian-style,
to do you in. The tricks
those rascals used to play. A nasty
lot, one as bad as another.

Dear Gorgo, what's to become of us?
The King's war-horses! Dear fellow,
don't ride me down. The brown one's
rearing. How wild he is! Get back,
Eunoa, you reckless girl. He'll kill
the man leading him. Lucky
I left baby at home.

Gorgo.   It's all right,
Praxinoa. We're past them now
and they've gone to their post.

Praxinoa.   And I'm pulling myself together
again too. I've been more scared
of a horse and a cold snake
than anything, since I was a girl.
Let's hurry. The crowd's swamping us.

Gorgo.   Have you come from the palace,
Mother?

Old Woman.   That I have, children.

Gorgo.   Is it easy to get in, then?

Old Woman.	The Greeks got into Troy by trying, pretty ones. Everything's done by trying.
Gorgo.	The old girl speaks her oracles, and off she goes.
Proxinoa.	Women know everything—even how Zeus married Hera.
Gorgo.	Look, Praxinoa, what a crowd there is at the doors!
Praxinoa.	Terrifying! Give me your hand, Gorgo. Eunoa, take Eutychis', and don't get separated from her. We must all go in together. Eunoa, stay close to us. O dear, Gorgo, my cloak's torn in two already. For god's sake, sir, if you hope for happiness, watch out for my cloak.
Man.	I'll try, but I'm almost helpless myself.
Praxinoa.	It's a real mob. They jostle each other like pigs.
Man.	Cheer up, lady. We're all right now.
Praxinoa.	I hope you'll be all right this year and forever, sir, for looking after us. What a nice, kind man! Eunoa's getting squashed. Come, you silly girl. Push! There. All inside, as the bridegroom said when he locked the bedroom door.
Gorgo.	Praxinoa, come look first at the tapestries. How delicate they are, and how beautiful— cloth for the gods.
Praxinoa.	Lady Athene! What weavers must have woven them,

and what artists painted them,
they're so lifelike. The figures
stand and turn so naturally,
they're alive, not woven. How ingenious
man is. And how wonderful *he* is,
lying there on his silver couch,
with the first down spreading
from his temples—thrice-loved
Adonis, loved even in Acheron.

Second Man.   Women, do stop that endless cooing.
Turtledoves! They'll bore one to death
with their broad vowels.

Praxinoa.   Well!
Where did this gentleman show up from?
And what's it to you if we chatter?
Order your own slaves about.
It's Syrakousan ladies
you're giving orders to now.
And I'll tell you another thing,
we're Korinthians by descent,
like Bellerophon. We speak
Peloponnesian, and Dorians
may speak Dorian, I suppose?
By Persephone, I'll not be ruled
by more than one master. And I won't
be bullied. Don't waste your threats on me.

Gorgo.   Quiet, Praxinoa. The Argive woman's
daughter's going to sing the *Adonis*—
the singer who won the prize
for dirge-singing last year.
She'll give us something fine,
I'm sure. Now she's clearing her throat.

The Woman sings: Goddess, lover of Idalion
and Golgi, and heights of Eryx,
golden Aphrodite, see—
after a year the Hours have brought you
Adonis, back from Acheron's stream.
The dear, soft-pacing Hours,
tardiest of the immortals—
yet blessed is their coming,
bringing gifts to all men.

Kyprian, child of Dione,
they say you changed Berenike
from mortal to immortal,
dropping sweet ambrosia
into her woman's breast.
Goddess of many names
and many temples, for you
Berenike's daughter Arsinoe,
lovely as Helena, pampers
Adonis with all good things.
Beside him in their season
all fruits the tall trees bear,
and fine plants in silver baskets,
and gold flasks of Syrian perfume.
All cakes, that women shape
in the kneading tray by mixing
colors with the white wheat-flour,
or make with sweet honey and oil.
All flying and creeping things
are there too, and green bowers
built for him, and covered
with tender dill. Boy-Loves
fly overhead, like fledgling
nightingales in the trees,
fluttering from bough to bough
to try their tender wings.
The ebony, the gold,
the eagles of white ivory
that carry to Zeus, the son
of Kronos, the darling boy
who pours him out his wine.
Crimson coverlets above,
soft as sleep. Miletos
will say, and he who pastures
his flocks in Samos "Ours
the covers for Adonis' bed."
In Adonis' rosy arms
the Kyprian, and he in hers.
Of eighteen or nineteen years
is the bridegroom. Golden down
is still on his lip. His kisses
do not scratch. Goodnight to Kypris,

lying in her lover's arms.
But at daybreak, with the dew,
we'll carry him all together
out to the waves that break
on the shore. And there, with loosened
hair, and breasts bare, and robes
falling to the ankles, begin
our song, high-pitched and clear.
You alone, dear Adonis,
of the demigods, men say,
visit both earth and Acheron.
On Agamemnon fell not
the choice, nor mighty Aias,
hero of heavy anger,
nor upon Hektor, the eldest
of Hekabe's twenty sons.
Nor on Patrokles, nor Pyrrhos
when he came back from Troy,
nor the Lapiths of old days,
nor Deukalion and his race.
Nor on the house of Pelops
and Pelasgian lords of Argos.

Look favorably upon us
now and throughout the year,
dear Adonis. Happy has your coming
been, Adonis, and happy
will it be when you come again.

Gorgo.   Praxinoa, the woman's cleverer
than we knew—happy woman
to know so much, and happiest
of all to have such a voice.
Still, it's time to go home.
Diokleides hasn't had his dinner,
and the man's all vinegar—
don't go near him when he's hungry.
Forewell, beloved Adonis.
Come make us happy again soon.

SIXTEENTH IDYLL

It is always the task of Zeus's daughters
and of poets to praise the immortals
and the deeds of noble men. The Muses
are gods. Being gods, they sing of gods.
But we're men. Being men, let's sing of men.
Who of all that live under the blue morning
will open his doors to receive my Graces
gladly, and not send them back empty-handed?
For then they come home barefoot and frowning
and abuse me at length because their journey
was profitless, and once again lie shamed,
heads bent over cold knees, at the bottom
of an empty box, where they always go
when they come back unsuccessful.
Where is there such a person today?
Who will cherish the one who sings his praises?
I don't know, for men no longer seek praise
for noble deeds, but are slaves of profit,
and every man has his hand in his pocket,
looking to see where he can win more silver,
and won't rub even the rust from it
to give away, but quickly replies:
"The shin is further than the knee. What's in it
for me? Let the gods take care of poets.
Who needs another poet? Homer
is enough for everyone. The best poet
is the one who gets nothing from me."
Deluded men, what good do you get
from the gold lying there uncounted?
Riches give the wise man pleasure
not in this, but in being indulgent
to himself and perhaps to some poet.
He provides for many of his kinsmen
and for many others, and is always
sacrificing on the gods' altars.

And he never treats strangers badly,
but uses them kindly at his table
and sends them graciously home again
when they are ready to go. Above all
he honors the sacred interpreters
of the Muses. That way you'll have good fame
even when you're hidden in Haides,
instead of moaning on the cold shore
of Acheron unhonored, like one whose hands
are calloused from the spade—some poor man
bewailing his heritage of poverty.
Many slaves drew their monthly rations
in the palaces of Antiochos
and King Aleuas. Many lowing calves
were driven home with the horned cattle
to the cowpens of the Skopadai.
Ten thousand fine sheep were watched by shepherds
on the plane of Krannon, under the sky,
for the stranger-loving Kreondai.
Yet they had no pleasure in these things
once they had given their sweet spirits
to the grim old ferryman's great raft.
And leaving behind all their riches,
would have lain long ages unremembered
among the unfortunate dead,
if the glorious bard of Keios
hadn't sung his accomplished songs
to the many-stringed harp and made them
famous among men of later days.
Even the swift horses that came back
crowned from the sacred games achieved glory.
Who would know of the Lykian princes,
or Priamos' long-haired children, or Kyknos,
white-skinned as a woman, if poets
hadn't sung the old battles of heroes?
And even Odysseus would never
have won lasting fame, though he wandered
a hundred and twenty months among all kinds
of men, and came alive to farthest
Haides, and escaped the dread Kyklops' cave.
Eumaios, the swineherd, and Philoitios,
busy with the cattle of the herds,

and great-hearted Laertes himself
would have gone unnamed if the singing
of the Ionian hadn't blessed them.
Men may gain renown from the Muses,
but the wealth of the dead is squandered
by the living. Yet it's as easy
to count the waves on the beach, as the wind
drives them to land from the gray sea,
or wash a brick of clay in clear water,
as to reason with a man obsessed
with love of money. Goodbye to such men.
May they have more silver than they can count
and always burn with desire for more.
As for me, I'd rather have men's honor
and friendship than many mules and horses.
I'm seeking a place among mortals
where I may come as a welcome guest,
accompanied by the Muses.
For the ways of poets are difficult
who travel without the company
of great counsellor Zeus's daughters.
But the heavens have not grown weary
of driving on the months and the years.
And the horses will pull day's chariot
many times more. And the man
will appear who needs me for his poet
when he's done such deeds as Achilles
or terrible Aias, by the tomb
of Phrygian Ilos, on Simois' plain.
Even now the Phoinikians who live
on Libya's edge, beneath the setting sun,
shake with fear. Even now Syrakousans
grasp their spears by the middle and burden
their arms with wicker shields, while among them
Hiero girds himself like heroes of old,
his helmet shaded by the horsehair crest.
O Zeus, our famous father, and Mistress
Athene, and you, Maiden, to whom
with your mother belongs the great city
of the rich Ephyraians by the waters
of Lysimeleia—may an evil fate
drive our enemies from the island

over the Sardonian waves to tell
of their loved ones' deaths to children and wives—
survivors easy to count from so many.
And may all our towns spoiled by enemy hands
be peopled by their former citizens
again. May they work the fertile fields,
and may countless thousands of sheep fatten
in pastures and go bleating over the plain,
and may cattle coming home in herds
warn the late traveler to hurry
on his way. And may the fallow ground
be plowed at seed-time when the cicada
sings overhead in the treetops, watching
the shepherds in the sun. And may spiders
spin their slender webs over battle-weapons,
and the battle-cry be heard no more.

And may poets carry Hiero's fame
far beyond the Skythian sea
to the place where Semiramis built
the great wall and caulked it with pitch
and reigned inside. I'm but one. Zeus's daughters
love many others. May they all
choose to praise Sikelian Arethousa
with her people and her spearman, Hiero.

You Graces, goddesses whom Eteokles
loved—you that love Minyan
Orchomenos, hated by Thebes
in the old days—if no one invites me,
I'll stay at home. But to the houses
of those who call me I'll come
confidently, with my Muses.
I won't leave you behind, for what can men know
that's desirable, without the Graces.
With the Graces may I always live.

SEVENTEENTH IDYLL

Let us begin with Zeus and end with Zeus
in our songs, Muses, for he is greatest
among the immortals. But among men
let Ptolemaios be named first and last
and in between, for he is pre-eminent.
The heroes begotten by demigods
in the old days found skillful poets
when they had accomplished noble deeds,
and I must make a hymn for Ptolemaios,
since I have skill in praising, and hymns
are pleasing even to immortals.
The woodchopper coming to many-treed Ida
looks around him at all that plenty,
wondering where to begin his work.
And what shall I speak of first, of all
the innumerable graces the gods
have showered upon this best of kings?
How able, because of his lineage,
was Lagos' son, Ptolemaios,
to achieve mighty deeds when his mind
devised a plan no other man could conceive.
The Father has given him equal honor
with the immortals. A golden throne
is set up for him in the house of Zeus,
and beside him sits his friend Alexandros,
the Persians' scourge, god of the bright headdress.
Facing them, carved in stubborn adamant,
sits the chair of Herakles, centaur-slayer,
feasting with the other gods and rejoicing
exceedingly in his children's children.
For Kronos' son has taken away old age
from their limbs, and they, his progeny,
are called immortals. Herakles' strong son
was ancestor to both, and both trace back
their distant origins to Herakles.

Therefore, whenever he has drunk his fill
of nectar and is going from the feast
to the bedroom of his beloved wife,
he hands to one his bow and the quiver
which dangles from his arm, and to the other
his knobby iron club, and they escort him,
Zeus's bearded son, with his weapons,
to white-ankled Hebe's ambrosial chamber.

Again, how Berenike's fame shone forth
among discreet women, a great blessing
to her parents. Dione's daughter,
Kypros' queen, touched with her slender fingers
her sweet-smelling breasts, till men say
no woman ever brought man such delight
as Ptolemaios found in love for his wife.
Yet he was loved by her even more.
And when a man goes loving to the bed
of a wife who loves him in return,
he may safely trust his house to his children.
But the unloving wife sets her mind
on other men, and though she bears children
freely, they won't take after the father.
Aphrodite, queen of the goddesses,
and most beautiful, she was your care.
By your grace, lovely Berenike
escaped the crossing of Acheron,
river of mourning, for you snatched her away
before she came to the black ship
and the ever-hateful ferryman of dead souls,
and set her up in your temple and gave her
a share of your worship. She is kindly
to all mortals, and inspires gentle loves,
and lightens the cares of longing ones.

The dark-eyebrowed maid of Argos bore
killer Diomedes, in marriage
with Tydeus, the man of Kalydon.
Deep-bosomed Thetis bore spearman Achilles
to Peleus, Aiakos' son. But you,
warrior Ptolemaios, famed Berenike
bore to warrior Ptolemaios. And Kos
received you, a new-born babe from your mother,
and nursed you when you first saw the dawn.

For it was there that Antigone's daughter,
heavy with pain, cried to Eileithuia,
loosener of girdles, who stood beside her
to give help and spread through all her limbs
relief from suffering. And there was born
a lovely child, the image of his father.
And Kos cried out for joy, when she saw him,
and touched the child with gentle hands, and said:
"Blessings upon you, boy. Honor me
as Phoibos Apollo honored Delos
of the dark snood. Bring similar renown
to the hill of Triopon, and extend
your favor to our Dorian neighbors,
as lord Apollo loved Rhenaia too."
The island spoke thus, and from the clouds
overhead a great eagle, bird of fate,
screamed three times—a sign from Zeus, surely,
for Zeus, son of Kronos, has in his care
all great kings, but especially the one
he has loved from birth. Much wealth is his,
and he rules many lands and many seas.

Ten thousand countries and ten thousand tribes
ripen their crops with the help of Zeus's rain,
but none is so fertile as Aigyptos' plain
when overflowing Neilos soaks the soil
and loosens it. None has so many towns
full of men skilled in crafts. Three hundred
cities are built there, and three thousand,
and three times ten thousand, and twice three
and three times nine besides, and great Ptolemaios
is king of them all. And he takes for himself
a part of Phoinikia and Arabia,
and of Syria and Libya,
and the black Aithiopians. He rules
all the Pamphylians and Kilikians,
the Lykians and war-loving Karians,
and the islands of the Kyklades.
For his ships are the best that sail the seas,
and all the seas and lands and roaring rivers
acknowledge Ptolemaios' reign. Many horsemen
and many foot-soldiers clad in shining bronze
gather round him. In riches he outweighs

67

all kings, so many things come every day
to his splendid palace from every side.

His people carry on their trades in peace.
No enemy from the land crosses the Neilos,
teeming with monsters, to raise the battle-cry
in villages not his own. And none
leaps armed from his swift ship upon the shore
to harry Aigyptos' cattle, so great a man
is throned in those level plains—Ptolemaios,
gold-haired, skilled spearman. Like a good king,
he is determined to hold everything
inherited from his fathers and to add
something of his own. Yet the piles of gold,
like the stores of ever-toiling ants,
do not lie useless in that rich house.
The glorious temples of the gods
receive much, for he offers first-fruits
and many other gifts, and he gives
much to mighty kings, much to cities,
and much to his loyal friends. No singer
skilled in raising his clear-voiced song
comes to Dionysos' sacred contests
without receiving the gift his art deserves.
And these interpreters of the Muses
sing of Ptolemaios for his kindnesses.
What can be finer for a wealthy man
than to win good fame among men?
Even for Atreus' sons that endures,
while the countless treasures won when Priamos'
great house was sacked lie hidden somewhere
in that mist from which there is no return.

He alone, from all the men of old
and those whose footprints are still warm
in the dust molded by their feet, has built
incensed temples for his dear mother
and father. There he has set them up
in beautiful gold and ivory
to be the helpers of all mankind.
And he burns many fat oxen's thighs
on the reddening altars as the months
go round, he and his stately wife.

No finer woman ever embraced her bridegroom
in his halls, loving with all her heart
her brother and husband. In like manner
was accomplished the holy marriage
of the immortals Queen Rhea bore
to rule Olympos. Ever-virgin Iris
strews with myrrh-washed hands a single bed
for the sleeping of Zeus and Hera.
Farewell, prince Ptolemaios. I will speak
of you as of the other demigods,
and what I say of you will not be lost,
I think, on men who live hereafter.
But for great deeds, you must pray to Zeus.

EIGHTEENTH IDYLL

Once in Sparta, to fair-haired Menelaos' house
came maidens with hyacinth blossoms in their hair—
twelve of them, the first of the town and loveliest
of the Lakonian girls. There they made ready
for the dance outside the new-painted bridal-room,
after Atreus' younger son had locked its door
on Helena, Tyndareos' child, whom he wooed
and won. Then in unison they sang, beating time
with weaving feet. The house rang with their marriage song.
Dear bridegroom, have you fallen asleep already?
Are you so heavy-limbed, so eager for sleeping?
Or had you drunk too much, when you cast yourself down
on your bed? If you wanted to sleep so early,
you should have slept by yourself, and left the maiden
with her maidens at her mother's side, to play
till early dawn. Tomorrow, and its tomorrow,
year after year, Menelaos, she is your bride.

O happy bridegroom, somebody sneezed for your luck
when you came with the other princes to Sparta,
and you alone of the demigods shall have Zeus,
son of Kronos, for father-in-law. His daughter,
an Achaian maiden such as whom no other
walks the earth, has come beneath the same coverlet
with you. And she will bear you a wonderful child
if it looks like its mother. For we, all maidens
her age, have run together, anointed like men,
by the baths of Eurotas—four times sixty girls,
and none was without a fault, except Helena.

A beautiful face the rising dawn discloses,
o mistress Night, or the bright spring when winter
ends, and so among us golden Helena shone.
As crops springing up make lovely the rich plowland,
or tall cypress the garden, or Thessalian
horse the chariot, rosy Helena adorns

Lakedaimon. No one else winds from her basket
such wool, or weaves with her shuttle at the carved loom
and cuts from the tall loom-beams a closer fabric.
Nor does anyone else strike with such skill the lyre,
hymning Artemis and broad-bosomed Athene,
as Helena, within whose eyes is all desire.

Beautiful, graceful maiden, you're a housewife now,
but we will go out early to the running-place
and grass-fields, gathering bunches of sweet flowers,
thinking of you still, Helena, as young lambs long
for the teats of their mother. First we'll weave for you
a crown of ground-lotus to hang from a plane-tree's
shady boughs. And for you we'll take smooth oil and drip it
from a silver flask beneath the shady plane-tree.
And we'll write on its bark, so passers-by may read,
in Dorian: "Worship me. I'm Helena's tree."

Goodnight, bride. Goodnight bridegroom, son of a mighty
father. Leto, nurse Leto, grant you fine children.
Kypris, goddess Kypris, grant equal love. And Zeus,
Kronos' son Zeus, grant unending prosperity,
passing down from noble fathers to noble sons.

Sleep, breathing love and desire in each other's breast,
but do not forget to wake at dawn. We will come
again before daylight when the earliest cock
raises his brightly-feathered neck from sleep to crow.

Hymen, o Hymenaios, joy in this marriage.

NINETEENTH IDYLL

One day a wicked bee
stung thievish Eros when he
was stealing honey from the hive,
and pricked his finger-tips.
He was in pain, and blew
on his hand, and danced up and down,
and stamped on the ground.
And he showed his hurt to Aphrodite,
and complained that so little a creature
as a bee could inflict so mighty
a wound. But his mother laughed.
"Aren't you like the bees—so little
to inflict such mighty wounds?"

TWENTIETH IDYLL

Eunika laughed when I wanted
to kiss her sweetly, and mocking me,
she said "Get away from me.
Fool, what makes you think you can kiss me—
you, a cowherd? I've never learned
to kiss country-style, but only
to press lips with city-folk. Don't you dare
kiss my pretty mouth, even in dreams.
How you look, and how you talk!
What coarse manners you have!
Is your voice so delicate,
your conversation so refined,
your beard so soft? Why, your mouth
is diseased, your hands black,
and you stink! Go away.
You'll get me dirty!" That's the way
she spoke to me, and she spat
three times into her bosom,
and looked me over from head to foot,
pouting her lips and glancing
with half-shut eyes. And she wriggled
her body, and sneered, and laughed
at me. Immediately
my blood boiled and I turned
as red as a dewy rose
under the sting. Off she went
and left me, but deep in my heart
I'm angry that a wretched whore
scorned a handsome fellow like me.

Tell me the truth, shepherds.
Don't you think I'm good-looking?
Has some god changed me suddenly
from the man I was? Until now,
beauty flowered upon me like ivy

on a tree, and covered my chin,
and my hair curled round my temples
like parsley, and my forehead
shone white above my dark eyebrows.
My eyes were brighter by far
than the glance of gray-eyed Athene,
my mouth was softer than curds,
and from it my voice flowed sweeter
than honey from the honeycomb.
And my music is sweet, too,
whether I play tunes on the pipe
or improvise on the flute,
or the reed, or the flageolet.
All the mountain-girls call me handsome
and give me kisses—all of them.
But this town-girl won't kiss me,
because I'm a cowherd, and runs
away, and won't listen.
Didn't handsome Dionysos
herd calves in the valleys? And doesn't
she know how Kypris lost her mind
over a herdsman, and drove cattle
on the Phrygian hills, and loved
Adonis among the thickets,
and mourned him among the thickets?
Who was Endymion? Wasn't he
a cowherd whom Selene loved,
as he grazed his cattle, and came
down from Olympos to the grove
of Latmos to lie with the boy?
And you, Rhea, weep for your cowherd.
And didn't you, son of Kronos,
take the form of a wandering bird
for a herding boy? Only Eunika
won't kiss a cowherd, and is greater
than Kybele and Kypris and Selene.
May she never again, Kypris,
kiss her darling, whether in town
or among the hills. But let her
sleep by herself all night long.

TWENTY-FIRST IDYLL

Poverty alone, Diophantes,
wakens the crafts. It's from her
men learn to work, for a working man
is prevented even from sleeping
by tiresome cares. If he closes
his eyes for a while in the night,
worries come crowding upon him
suddenly, to break up his rest.
Two old fishermen lay together
on a bed made of dried seaweed
in their wattled hut, leaning
against the leafy wall. The tools
of their trade were lying nearby—
baskets, reed poles, hooks and weedy nets,
lines and traps and lobster-pots
of woven rushes, ropes, oars,
and an old rowboat on its props.
A thin mat beneath their heads,
their clothes, their caps—these were all
their wealth—all they had to show
for their labor. They had no key,
no door, no watchdog, nor any need
for such things. Poverty guarded them,
they had no neighbors, and the sea
surrounded them, gently surging
to the very walls of their cabin.
The moon's chariot hadn't reached
the middle point in its journey
when their customary labor
roused the fishermen, wiped their eyes
of sleep, and stirred their thoughts to speech.

Asphalion. They lied, my friend, when they said
the nights grow short in summer
because they bring the long days.

Though it's not yet dawn, I've had
ten thousand dreams. Am I mistaken,
or why are these nights so long?

Friend. Why blame the lovely summertime,
Asphalion? It's not the season,
willfully wandering from its course,
but worry that cuts short your sleep
and makes the night seem longer.

Asphalion. Have you ever learned to read dreams?
I've had a fine one, and I wouldn't
want you not to share in it.

Friend. We share our catch and we ought to share
all our dreams. I'll use common sense
and guesswork. The best interpreter's
the one who learns from his wits.
Besides, we've plenty of time,
for what's there for us to do,
lying on a leafy pallet
wide awake by the sea? They say
the donkey in the thornbush and the lamp
in the townhall never sleep.
Tell me your night's vision. A friend
should always be told a man's dreams.

Asphalion. Last night, when I fell asleep
after our sea work (and not overfed,
for we ate early, you remember,
and didn't overtax our stomachs),
I saw myself busy on a rock,
sitting and watching for fish,
dangling my bait at the pole's end.
And a big one nibbled at it
(sleeping dogs dream of bread, and I
of fish). Then he was hooked, and bled.
As he struggled, my pole bent
in my hand, and I pulled and strained
and wondered how to land the big fish
with such weak gear. But I pricked him
to remind him of the hook,
and gave him some line, but then,
when he didn't run, took in slack.
The battle was over. I landed
a golden fish—a fish all covered

with thick gold. Then I was afraid
he was a favorite fish of Poseidon
or some cherished possession
of sea-green Amphitrite.
And I unhooked him carefully
lest the barbs pull away some gold
from his mouth, swearing I'd never
again set foot upon the sea
but stay ashore and be a king
with my gold. That woke me up.
Now, friend, apply your mind to it,
for I'm frightened by the oath I swore.

Friend.   Don't let that scare you. You neither
swore the oath nor caught the gold fish
you dreamed of. All dreams are lies.
But if you'll search these waters,
awake, not asleep, there's hope
something will come of your dreaming.
Hunt real fish, or you'll perish
of hunger and your golden dreams.

TWENTY-SECOND IDYLL

We praise the sons of Leda and aegis-bearing
  Zeus—
Kastor, and Polydeukes, dangerous boxer
when he straps his knuckles with the oxhide
  thongs.
Twice and three times we sing of the children
born to Thestios' daughter, two Spartan brothers
who give help to men on the edge of disaster,
and horses panicked in bloody battle, and ships
which, defying the stars as they rise and set
in the sky, meet terrible storms—gusts that raise
huge waves astern, or ahead, or wherever
they will and hurl them into the hold and smash
the planking on either side. Then sails and shrouds
hang tangled together and torn, and night comes,
and heavy rains fall from heaven, and the wide
  sea
roars, whipped by winds and iron hail. Yet even
  then
you draw forth ships and sailors from the depths
when they had been expecting to die. And the
  winds
become still, and oily calm covers the sea,
and the clouds scatter, blowing this way and that.
Then the Bears appear, and the Manger, dimly
  seen
between the Asses, telling all's clear for sailing.

Twin helpers of mortals, much-loved pair—
horsemen, harpers, athletes, bards—shall I sing
  first
of Kastor or of Polydeukes? I'll praise
them both, but first I'll sing of Polydeukes.

The Argo had safely passed the clashing rocks
and the dangerous mouth of snowy Pontos

and come, carrying the dear sons of the gods,
to the land of the Bebrykes. There the heroes
from both sides of Iason's ship disembarked
by one ladder, and setting foot on the wide beach,
spread bed-litter and took firesticks in their hands
on the sheltered shore. But Kastor of the fast
   horses
and dark-faced Polydeukes wandered away
from their comrades to explore the woods together
where trees of all sorts grew wild on the hillside.
Beneath a smooth rock they found a brimming
   spring
with water that was always clear. At the bottom
pebbles shone like crystal or silver. Tall pines
   grew
beside it, and poplars, planetrees, and cypresses,
and all the sweet-smelling flowers that fill meadows
in late spring, loved and harvested by hairy bees.
A giant man was sitting there in the sun.
He was terrible to look at: his ears were crushed
by hard fists, his heavy chest and broad back
bulged with iron flesh, like a hammered metal
   statue,
and the muscles on his arms beneath the shoulders
stood out like round stones rolled smooth by winter torrents
in their swirling eddies. A lion's skin
was slung over his back and neck, hung by its
   claws.
Champion Polydeukes accosted him first:

Polydeukes. Good day, sir, whoever you are. Whose land is
     this?

Amykos. What's good about it, when I see strangers before
     me?

Polydeukes. Don't worry. I promise we're not thieves or
     thieves' sons.

Amykos. I won't worry. But I don't need you to tell me so.

Polydeukes. Are you a savage, always resentful and proud?

Amykos. I'm what you see, and no trespasser on your land.

Polydeukes.   Come there with us, and you'll bring home gifts of friendship.

Amykos.   I don't want your gifts, and I've none to give you.

Polydeukes.   Well, sir, won't you even let us drink this water?

Amykos.   You'll find that out when thirst burns your shriveled lips.

Polydeukes.   Will silver persuade you, then, or what is your price?

Amykos.   Put up your fists and fight, face to face, man to man.

Polydeukes.   Boxing? Or foot-fighting too, and eye for eye?

Amykos.   Fists. And you won't have to pull your punches.

Polydeukes.   Who is it, then, with whom I'll mix fists and thongs?

Amykos.   You're looking at him. I'm called boxer, not woman.

Polydeukes.   But do we fight each other for a prize?

Amykos.   I'll be called yours, or you mine, if I beat you.

Polydeukes.   Those are the terms on which red-combed game-cocks fight.

Amykos.   Gamecocks or lions, we fight for no other prize.
Amykos said this, and seized a hollow shell
and blew on it, and at the sound of the shell
the long-haired Bebrykes gathered quickly
under the shady planetrees. And Kastor,
the brave fighter, also went and summoned
all the heroes from the Magnesian ship.
When they both had braced their fists with leather thongs
and wound the long straps around their arms, they stepped
into the center together, ready to kill
one another, and busily maneuvered
to see which one could get the sun at his back.
But Polydeukes' skill outdid the big man,
and the rays fell directly in Amykos' face.
Then he rushed in, hot and angry, sparring
with his fists. But Tyndareos' son caught him
on the point of the chin as he came in,

angering him still more, till his attack
became confused and he charged, head down,
with all his strength. The Bebrykes cheered,
and from the other side the heroes shouted
encouragement to brave Polydeukes,
afraid that Tityos-like man would crush him
with his weight and defeat him in that narrow
    place.
But Zeus's son, shifting this way and that,
cutting him with rights and lefts, broke the
    charge
of Poseidon's overbearing son
till he stood reeling with blows and spitting blood.
And all the heroes shouted when they saw
the terrible cuts around his mouth and jaws
and the way his face swelled till his eyes were
    slits.
Then the prince teased him with feints from all
    sides
and when he saw him fuddled, drove with his fist
to the brow above the middle of the nose
and laid open the forehead to the bone.
With that blow, he lay stretched on his back
among the flowers and the grass.
When he rose again, there was vicious fighting,
as they punished each other with the heavy
    thongs.
The Bebrykes' chief kept landing on the chest
and neck, while invincible Polydeukes
kept smashing at the face with disfiguring blows.
The flesh of the one melted away with sweat
till he shrunk from a big man to a small one,
but the other's limbs kept growing stronger
and his color better as he got down to work.
How at last, then, did the son of Zeus flatten
that glutton? Tell, goddess, for you know, and I,
interpreting you to others, will utter
what you will, in whatever manner you please.
Now the giant, eager for some great stroke,
seized Polydeukes' left hand with his own,
and stooping sidewise under his guard, let fly
with the other, driving his huge fist upward

from his right side. If the blow had landed,
it would have done great harm to Amyklai's king,
but he ducked his head aside, and with his right
    fist
struck below the left temple, putting his shoulder
into the blow. And dark blood spurted suddenly
from the gaping temple. With his left, he struck
at the mouth, rattling the close-set teeth, and
    mauled
the face with a quickening rain of blows
till the cheeks were smashed. Dizzy, he went
    down
in a heap and held up both hands, refusing
to fight anymore, for he was close to death.
Then, boxer Polydeukes, you did nothing
malicious, in spite of your victory.
But he swore you a mighty oath, calling upon
his father Poseidon in the sea, never
to do violence to strangers anymore.
Now, prince, I've sung your praise, and I'll sing
    of you,
Kastor, Tyndareos' son, master of horses,
wielder of the spear, bronze-armored warrior.
Zeus's two sons had seized Leukippos' daughters
and were carrying them off, but two brothers,
Lynkeus and great Idas, Aphareus' sons,
bridegrooms about to be married, pursued them
eagerly. When they came to Aphareus' tomb,
they leaped from their chariots all together,
and sprang at each other, weighed down with
    spears and shields.
Then Lynkeus spoke, shouting from under his
    helmet:
"Foolish men, why are you so eager for fighting,
and why so violent with other men's brides,
and why these naked weapons in your hands?
Leukippos pledged us his daughters long ago,
and the betrothal was confirmed with an oath.
It wasn't right, in order to steal the brides
of other men, for you to change his purpose
with gifts of cattle and mules and other things,
and cheat us of our weddings with your bribes.

I'm not a man of many words, but often
I've said to your faces 'Friends, this isn't the way
for heroes to win wives, when they've grooms
    already.
Sparta is large, and so is horse-breeding Elis,
and sheep-rich Arkadia, and the cities
of Achaia and Messene and Argos,
and all the seacoast of Sisyphos. Ten thousand
maidens live there, in the homes of their parents,
lacking neither beauty nor intelligence,
and you could easily marry any you choose,
for many would be glad to be fathers-in-law
to noble men, and you are pre-eminent
among all the heroes, you and your fathers
and your fathers' families from the old days.
Therefore, friends, let us carry out this wedding
as planned, and together we'll find you another.'
I spoke this way many times, but the wind's
    breath
carried away my words to the wet sea-waves,
and my speeches had no effect. For you're both
hard, stubborn men. Yet listen to me even now.
You're both our cousins on the father's side.
But if your hearts are set on war, and a cousins'
quarrel must end in battle, and we must bathe
our spears in blood, let Idas and his cousin,
mighty Polydeukes, hold off from the fighting,
while Kastor and I, the younger born, decide
the quarrel. Let us not leave to our parents
a greater sorrow. One killed from each family
is enough. The others will feast their friends
together as bridegrooms, not as corpses,
and marry these girls. Great strife will end with
    small loss."
He said this, and the god chose not to let him
speak in vain. The older pair laid down their
    armor
from off their shoulders, but Lynkeus stepped
    forth
to the center, shaking his spear beneath the rim
of his shield, and Kastor leveled his spear-point
in like manner, and the horsehair plumes nodded

on each man's crest. They worked first with their spears,
thrusting at each other whenever they saw
a piece of naked flesh. But before either one
could deliver a wound, the spear-points were stuck fast
in the thick shields, and broken. Then they drew their swords
from their sheaths, and tried again to kill each other,
with no break in the fighting. And Kastor landed
many blows on the broad shield and horsehair crest,
and sharp-eyed Lynkeus struck many on the shield,
and his point sheared off the crimson plume. But then,
as Lynkeus aimed his sharp sword at the knee,
Kastor stepped back with his left foot and hacked off
his fingers. Lynkeus, stricken, dropped his sword
and quickly turned to escape to his father's tomb,
where brave Idas lay, watching this war of kins-men.
But Tyndareos' son went racing after him
and thrust with his broad sword through side and navel,
and instantly the bronze severed the bowels,
and Lynkeus bowed and fell forward on his face,
and heavy sleep rushed down upon his eyelids.

Nor did Laokoosa see her other son
happily married, either, at his father's hearth,
for quickly Idas of Messene tore up
the gravestone from Aphareus' tomb to throw it
at his brother's killer, but Zeus protected him,
and struck the carved stone from his enemy's hands,
and consumed him with a fiery lightning-bolt.

It's no small matter to quarrel with the sons
of Tyndareos, for they are powerful men,
and the sons of a powerful father.
Farewell, children of Leda. Send us good fame

for our singing. All singers are dear to the sons
of Tyndareos, and Helena, and the other
heroes who helped Menelaos sack Ilios.
The Chian singer brought you glory, princes,
when he sang of Priamos' city and the ships
of the Achaians and Ilios' battles
and Achilles, tower in the fight. I too
bring you the clear-voiced Muses' sweet songs,
such as they provide, and all I have in store.
And for the gods the finest of gifts is song.

TWENTY-THIRD IDYLL

A lovesick man longed for a cruel youth,
beautiful in form but not in his manner,
for he hated his lover, and felt for him
no tenderness. He knew nothing of Eros—
what god he is, or what kind of bow
he carries, or what bitter arrows
he lodges in the heart. He was unyielding
whenever they met and spoke. There was
no solace for love's fires: no quivering
of the lips, or eye-glances, or blushing cheek—
not a word, not a kiss, to ease the passion.
Like a wild animal of the forest
watching the hunter, he looked at the man,
with hostile lip, and eyes that glared at him
as sternly as fate. His bitter mood
changed his whole face, which lost its color
because of his angry pride. Yet even so
he was handsome, and his haughtiness
moved the lover all the more, till at last
he could no longer bear so fierce a flame
of the Kythereian, but came and wept
by the cruel dwelling, and kissed the doorpost,
and lifted up his voice: "Cruel boy,
and heartless, a fierce lioness' nursling—
boy of stone, unworthy of love, I have come
with this last gift for you, my hanging-rope.
I will not anger you anymore, my boy,
with the sight of me, but will take the road
to which you have condemned me, where, men say,
is the common cure for lovers—oblivion.
But if with my lips I drain it, every drop,
even then I shall not quench my desire.
But now at last I bid farewell to your door.
I know what is to be. The rose is lovely,
but time withers it. And the violet

is beautiful in spring but grows old quickly.
The lily is white. It fades as it flowers.
And snow is white, until it melts on the ground.
The brightness of youth is beautiful, but lives
only a little while. The day will come
when you'll love, and your heart will burn, and you'll
   weep
salt tears. But my child, do me one last favor.
When you come out and find me, a poor wretch,
hanging in your doorway, don't pass me by,
but stay and weep awhile in libation,
and take me down from the rope, and cover me
with some clothing from your body. And give me
a last kiss, granting the grace of your lips
to the dead. Don't be afraid of me.
I can't harm you, reconciled with a kiss.
Dig me a grave to hide my love in
and before you go, cry over me three times
'Rest, my friend.' And also, if you will,
'My good friend is dead.' And write this epitaph
that I will scratch on your wall: 'This man
was killed by Love. Traveler, do not pass by,
but stop and say, He had a cruel friend.' "

When he had said this he took a stone
and set it in the middle of the doorway—
a terrible stone. And tied up the slender rope
and fastened the loop around his neck and kicked
the stone from under his foot and hung there dead.

But when the other opened the door
and saw the body hanging from his doorway,
his heart was unmoved, and he did not weep
for this strange death or defile his boy's clothes
on the corpse, but went off to the contests
at the gymnasium, light-heartedly
seeking his favorite bathing-place.
And there he met the god he had scorned,
on a stone pedestal above the water.
And the statue leaped on him, and killed
that cruel boy. The water reddened
with blood and the boy's voice floated above it:
"Rejoice, lovers, for the hater is dead.
And love, haters, for the god knows how to judge."

TWENTY-FOURTH IDYLL

When Herakles was ten months old,
Alkmena the Midean took him
and Iphikles, his younger brother
by one night, and laid them both,
washed and full of milk, in the shield
of bronze—a fine piece of armor—
which Amphitryon had taken
from Pterelaos when he fell.
And she touched the boys' heads, saying
"Sleep sweetly, my little ones,
and wake again. Sleep, my darlings,
two brothers unharmed. Rest happily,
and happily meet the dawn."
With these words she rocked the great shield,
and quickly sleep came over them.
But when the Bear at midnight
swings westward opposite Orion,
where he shows his mighty shoulder,
crafty Hera sent forth two monsters,
two blue-coiled, writhing serpents,
toward the wide threshold where the pillars
of the open doorway stood,
and commanded them to devour
the child Herakles. They writhed along,
uncoiling their bloodthirsty bellies
on the ground, and as they came,
an evil fire flashed from their eyes,
and they spat out deadly poison.
But when, with flickering tongues, they drew
    near
the boys, Alkmena's dear babies
awoke, for Zeus knew all, and light
shone through the house. Then Iphikles,
when he caught sight of the monsters
over the rim of the hollow shield

and saw their cruel teeth, began screaming
and kicked off the woollen covers,
eager to escape. But Herakles
confronted them, seized them with his hands,
and squeezed them both violently,
holding onto their throats, where vile snakes
carry their hateful venom, abhorred
even by the gods. Then around
the young boy, the unweaned child
who never cried, they wound their coils,
but their spines went limp with pain,
trying to escape that iron grip.

Alkmena heard the cry and woke first.
"Get up, Amphitryon. I'm frozen
with terror. Get up. Don't wait
to put on your shoes. Don't you hear
how loud the younger boy's screaming?
Haven't you noticed it's midnight,
yet all the walls are as bright
as if it were daybreak? There's something
strange in the house, dear husband,
I know there is." At her words
he got out of bed and quickly seized
his richly decorated sword
which always hung from its peg
above his bed of cedarwood.
And just as he was reaching out
for his newly woven sword-belt,
lifting with his other hand the sheath,
a mighty piece of lotus-wood,
darkness filled the large bedroom again.

Then he called out to his servants
as they lay, snoring heavily,
"Bring light, quickly, from the hearth,
my servants, and thrust back the strong
door-bolts." "Get up, faithful servants,
the master calls," cried a woman
of Phoinikia who slept
by the millstones. And they came
running with lighted torches,
and the house was filled with hurrying
people. And when they saw the child

Herakles clutching the two snakes
in his tender fists, they all
cried out and struck their hands together.
But he held out the creeping things
for his father, Amphitryon,
to see, and jumped up and down
in childish pleasure, and laughed,
and laid at his father's feet
the dread monsters, asleep in death.
Then Alkmena caught Iphikles
to her bosom, rigid with fright
and violently upset.
But Amphitryon laid the other boy
under the lamb's-wool coverlet
and went back to bed, thinking of sleep.

The cocks were crowing their third welcome
to the first faint dawn when Alkmena
summoned the seer Teiresias,
who speaks all the truth, and told him
the strange thing, and bade him tell her
what would come of it. "If the gods
intend some evil, do not hide it
out of sympathy for me.
For mortals can never escape
what Fate reels from her spindle.
But you know already, o seer,
son of Eueres, what I tell you."

The queen said this, and he answered:
"Take courage, daughter of Perseus,
mother of noble children.
Take courage, and treasure in your heart
promise of the better things to come,
for by the sweet light that long ago
left these eyes of mine, I tell you
many an Achaian woman,
carding the soft wool about her knees,
shall sing at evening of Alkmena
by name, and you will be honored
among the women of Argos,
so great a man shall go up
to starry heaven—this same son
of yours, a broad-chested hero,

master of all beasts and all men.
He is fated to accomplish
twelve labors and dwell in the house
of Zeus, but a pyre in Trachis
shall hold the mortal part of him.
From his bride, he shall be called
son of immortals—the same
who sent forth these serpents from the earth
to destroy the child. And the day
shall come when the fierce wolf, spying
the sleeping fawn, will not try
to do it harm. But woman,
you must have fire ready,
under the ashes, and dry sticks
of thorn, or bramble, or briar,
or wild pearwood, weather-beaten,
and on that wild firewood, burn
these two snakes at midnight—the hour
when they would have killed your child.
And at dawn have one of your maids
gather the ashes from the fire
and carry them beyond your borders,
over the river, every trace,
and scatter them among the broken rocks,
and come home without looking back. But first,
purify your house with sulphur smoke,
and according to the custom,
sprinkle clear water mixed with salt
from a branch wrapped around with wool
over everything. Sacrifice
a male pig to Zeus the Master,
so you may always have mastery
over your enemies." Saying this,
Teiresias, in spite of his years,
pushed back his ivory chair and went.

And Herakles, known as the son
of Amphitryon the Argive,
grew, under his mother's care,
like a sapling in the garden.
Letters old Linos taught the boy—
his watchful tutor, Apollo's son.
To bend the bow and send the arrow

to the mark Eurytos taught him,
rich in ancestral fields.
And Philammon's son, Eumolpos,
made him a singer and fitted
his two hands to the boxwood lyre.
All the tricks by which the hip-twisting
men of Argos throw each other
with their legs, and all devices
of boxers skilled with the hand-thongs,
and all that rough-and-tumble fighters
have devised to aid in their art
he learned from Harpalykos
of Panopeus, Hermes' son,
whom no one that saw him, even
at a distance, would await
with confidence in the ring,
so forbidding a brow overhung
his grim face. To drive his horses
in the chariot and to guide
the wheel-hub safely around
the turning-post, Amphitryon
himself taught his son with loving care,
for he had brought many prizes
back from swift races in Argos,
the grazing-land of horses,
and the chariots he rode in
remained unbroken till their thongs
loosened with age. How to attack
an enemy with spear at rest
and shield swung over the back,
how to withstand the biting swords,
order the battle-ranks, or measure
an advancing company
of foemen, or command horse-troops—
all this he learned from Kastor,
the cavalryman, who had come
into exile out of Argos
when Tydeus got from Adrastos
all his fields and his wide vineyards
in Argos, land of horses.
And no one was Kastor's equal
in fighting, among the demigods,

until age blunted his youth.
Such schooling his dear mother
found for Herakles, and the boy's bed
was set close to his father's—
a lion's skin which gave him
much delight. His dinner was roast meat
and a great Dorian loaf of bread
in a basket—more than enough
to satisfy a digging man.
But he had, at the day's end,
only a light supper, uncooked.
And his simple tunic reached
only a little below the knee.

TWENTY-FIFTH IDYLL

Then the old plowman who watched the cattle
answered him, interrupting the work
he had in hand: "I'll tell you gladly
what you ask, stranger, for I dread
the awful wrath of Hermes of the Roads.
He is the angriest of all the gods,
men say, if you refuse a traveler
who earnestly asks his way. The fleecy
flocks of King Augeias don't graze
all in one pasture, or one place.
Some feed on Helisous' banks, and others
by divine Alpheos' holy stream;
some in Bouprasion, rich in grapes,
and others right here. Separate pens
are built for each flock, but all his herds,
overflowing though they be, find pasture
without fail beside these great marshes
of Menios, for the dewy fields
and water-meadows grow plentiful crops
of sweet grass to provide the horned cattle
with strength. There on your right, in plain view,
stand the barns for all of them—over there
where the river runs and the planetrees
and green wild-olive trees grow thick—
a grove sacred to Apollo
of the Pastures, stranger, the most gracious
of the gods. Long rows of huts are built
nearby for us country folk who care
for the King's many marvelous possessions,
turning the fallow ground three or four times
in the sowing season. The boundaries
of his realm are known to the vine-tenders
who bring their harvests to the wine-vats
at the end of summer. For the whole plain
belongs to prudent Augeias—the wheatfields

and tree-filled orchards, all the way
to the uplands of Akroreia
with their springs. And all day long we work
busily upon them, as workmen
who live in the country always do.
But tell me now, for it will be
to your own advantage to do so,
who you're looking for. Augeias himself,
or one of his servants? I'll tell you
anything you want to know, for I see
from your well-proportioned body
you're not of common birth or manner.
I think the sons of the immortals
must look like you among mortal men."
Then Zeus's mighty son replied:
"You're right, old man, it's Augeias,
king of the Epeians, I'm looking for,
and it's need of him that brings me here.
But if he's in town with the citizens,
looking after his people and giving
judgments, then take me where I can see
one of his servants who's in charge here,
to explain my business and receive
an answer, for the gods have made men
dependent upon one another."
Then the good old plowman spoke again:
"Stranger, you must have been sent here
by one of the immortals, so quickly
things turn out the way you want them.
Helios' dear son, Augeias,
came here yesterday from the city
after many days, with Phyleus,
his noble and powerful son,
for an inspection of his countless wealth
in these parts. For kings, like other men,
seem to think their possessions are safer
if they keep an eye on them themselves.
But now we'll go to him. I'll take you
to my place, where we're likely to find him."
Saying this, he led the way, wondering
in his mind, as he studied the beast's skin
and the fist-filling club, where the stranger

came from. And time and time again
he wanted to ask, but kept catching
the words back as they sprang to his lips,
for fear he'd say something unsuitable,
considering his companion's hurry—
for it's hard to know another man's mind.
As they came near, the dogs, from far off,
suddenly became aware of them,
both by their scent and their footsteps, and rushed
from all directions, barking furiously,
at Herakles, Amphitryon's son.
But on the other side, they fawned
about the old man with meaningless yelping.
He scared them away by merely
picking up stones from the ground,
and threatened them all with his voice,
to stop their barking. But secretly
he was glad they protected his place
while he was away. Then he said
"What a hot-headed creature this is
that the gods, who rule everything,
have given man for a companion.
If he just had the intelligence
and good sense to know whom to quarrel with
and whom to leave alone, no animal
could compare with him in value.
But as it is, he's violent
and savage without reason." He said this,
and they walked rapidly to the dwelling.

Now Helios had turned his horses
to the west, bringing evening, and fat sheep
flocked in from the pastures to the farms
and pens. Next came cows by the thousands,
like rain-clouds rolling across the sky,
driven by the south wind or the north wind
from Thrake, passing without number or end,
so many new ones are rolled up
by the strong wind, wave after wave,
to join the old. In such numbers
the cattle-herds strung out behind,
till the whole plain was filled with homing cows—
the roads and the rich fields crowded

with their lowing. And the cowsheds
were soon filled with the shuffling creatures
and the sheep were settled in their pens.
Then no man, though there were so many,
stood idle among the cattle
for lack of work. One fastened clogs
to their feet with clean-cut leather thongs,
to make them stand still for milking.
Another set calves beneath their mothers,
eager to drink the warm milk. One held
a milk-pail, one set the rich cheese,
one led the bulls away from the heifers.
Augeias made the rounds of the stalls
to see what kind of care the herdsmen
were taking of his stock, and his son
and Herakles, powerful and wise,
accompanied the king as he passed
among his many possessions.

Then Amphitryon's son, though the spirit
in his breast was imperturbable
and always firm, marveled greatly
to see these countless gifts of the gods,
for no one would have said, or imagined
that one man's wealth could be so great—
or ten men's, even if they were richer
in flocks than all other kings. But Helios
had given his son this special gift,
that he should be rich above all others
in cattle, and he saw to it himself
that the herds increased steadily.
Augeias' stock escaped all sicknesses
that waste the herdsmen's labor. Each year
his horned cattle became more numerous
and better, for his cows bore more heifer-calves
than other men's, and never cast their young.

Three hundred white-legged bulls with curved horns
accompanied the herd, and two hundred
others that were red—all old enough
to mate with the cows. And besides these
there were twelve more, sacred to Helios.
These were white as swans, and outshone
all the other shambling beasts. They grazed

on the rich grass in a separate field,
too proud to mingle with the herds.
And whenever swift beasts came down
from the wild woods onto the plain
after the grazing cattle, these twelve
were first to catch their scent and attack them,
with murderous looks and fierce bellowing.
Among them, the first by far in strength,
power, and pride was mighty Phaethon,
whom all the herdsmen compared to a star
because he shone, bright and conspicuous,
as he moved among the other cattle.
Seeing the cured skin of a fierce lion,
he rushed at watchful Herakles
to drive his mighty head and forehead
into his side. But as he charged, the prince
grabbed his left horn with a strong hand,
bent his massive neck to the ground,
and thrust him back with his shoulder's weight,
while the muscles of his upper arm
strained and stood out above the sinews.
Then the king himself, and Phyleus,
his wise son, and the herdsmen tending
the horned cattle marveled to see
the great strength of Amphitryon's son.

Now Phyleus and mighty Herakles
left the rich fields to go to the town.
And when, by walking rapidly,
they reached the end of a narrow path,
barely visible in the green grass,
which ran through the vineyards from the farms,
and first set foot on the highway,
there Augeias' dear son, turning
his head slightly over his right shoulder,
addressed all-powerful Zeus's son,
who was walking behind him:
"Stranger, long ago I heard a story
which, now I think of it, may have been
about you. When I was a boy,
a man of Argos came this way—
an Achaian, from Helike
by the sea—and told a tale,

heard by many Epeians, of how,
in his presence an Argive had killed
a wild animal—a huge lion
that was scourging the countryside.
The monster lived in a hollow cave
near the grove of Nemean Zeus.
Whether the man was from holy Argos
or lived in the city of Tiryns
or in Mykene, he didn't know.
But he said, if I remember correctly,
he was descended from Perseus.

No one else of the Aigialeis,
I think, had courage for the deed
but you, and the beast's hide that covers
your sides shows clearly the prowess
of your hands. Come, hero, tell me first—
so I'll know whether my conjecture
is right or wrong—if you're the man
the Achaian of Helike
told us about, and I've guessed correctly.
Then tell me how you killed that terrible brute
single-handed, and how it ever got
to the well-watered land of Nemea,
for you won't find any such monsters
in Apia—nor would you want to—
for it doesn't nourish such great beasts,
but only boars and bears and fierce wolves.
That's why those who heard the story
were amazed, and some said the traveler
lied, to please his hearers with tall talk."

Saying this, Phyleus moved aside,
out of the middle of the roadway,
to make room for them to walk side by side,
and to hear better what Herakles
had to say. And he stepped up beside him
and said "Son of Augeias, you've answered
the first question readily and rightly
for yourself. As for that monster,
since you want to hear, I'll tell everything
that happened, except where it came from,
for of all the Argives, none can tell that
with certainty. We can only suppose

one of the immortals, angry
about some sacrifice, inflicted
this plague on Phoroneus' people.
For he overran all the lowlanders
without restraint, like a river in flood,
but most of all the Bembinians,
who lived near him and suffered terribly.
This was the first task required of me
by Eurystheus—to kill that savage beast.
So I set out, taking my supple bow
and my hollow quiver full of arrows,
and in my other hand a solid club
with the bark unstripped I had made
from a shady wild-olive I found
under sacred Helikon and pulled up—
the whole tree, tangled roots and all.
When I reached the place where the lion was,
I took my bow and slipped the bowstring
up to the curved tip, and notched to it
a deadly arrow, and looked this way
and that for the dangerous monster,
hoping I could discover him
before he caught sight of me. It was noon,
and I hadn't been able to find
his tracks or hear his roaring. Nor in all
those plowed fields was there anyone
busy with his cattle or farming
to be seen and questioned, since pale fear
kept everybody inside his door.
But I kept searching the leafy hill
and couldn't rest till I saw the beast
and put my strength at once to the test.
Along toward evening he was coming
to his cave, fed full of flesh and blood,
his rough mane and savage muzzle and chest
splashed with blood, still licking his jaws.
I hid quickly in the dark underbrush
beside the forest path, waiting
for his approach, and when he came nearer,
I hit him on the left flank, but that
was useless, for the sharp arrow
didn't pierce his flesh, but glanced off

and fell on the green grass. Instantly
he raised his bloody head from the ground
in amazement and glanced everywhere,
looking for me, his jaws open
and showing his ravenous teeth.
Then I sent another arrow
from the string, angry that the first one
had left my hand in vain. I hit him
squarely in the chest, where the lungs are,
but even then the cruel arrow
failed to penetrate his hide, and fell
uselessly in front of his feet.

Shamed and vexed in mind, I was going
to draw my bow for a third time,
when the pitiless brute looked around
and spied me. He lashed his long tail
against his sides, eager at once
for battle. His neck swelled with anger,
his tawny mane bristled with rage,
and his spine curved like a bow, as he drew
himself together about his flanks and loins.
Just as a chariot-maker, skilled
in many crafts, warms seasoned branches
of the figtree by the fire and bends them
to make rims for his chariot-wheels,
and as he bends it, the smooth-skinned figwood
flies from his hands and leaps far away
in one spring, that terrible lion
sprang upon me from a distance,
eager to feast himself on my flesh.

Then holding my arrows and the folded cloak
from my shoulders before me in one hand,
I raised my seasoned club above my head
with the other and brought it crashing down
on his skull. Square on the shaggy head
of that invincible beast, I broke
my tough olive club in two.
And before he could reach me, the lion
fell from the middle of his spring
to the ground, and stood there on weak legs,
shaking his head, as darkness gathered
in his two eyes and his brain was shaken

by the violent blow on his skull.
When I saw how the terrible pain
had dazed him, and before he could come to,
I seized him by the massive neck,
and dropping my bow and woven quiver
to the ground, choked him with all my strength,
gripping him with strong hands from behind,
lest he rip me with his claws, and treading
his hind feet into the ground with my heels,
while I pinned his sides with my thighs—
till I lifted his breathless body
upright in my arms and stretched it
on the ground, and vast Haides took his spirit.
After that, I wondered how to strip
the hairy skin from the dead beast's limbs,
a difficult task, for when I tried,
I couldn't cut it with iron or stone
or wood. But one of the immortals
put it into my mind to rip the skin
of the lion with its own claws.
With these I quickly flayed it and wrapped it
around my body to protect me
from the gashes and bruises of war.
That, my friend, was the end of the beast
of Nemea, which till then had brought
such woes upon animals and men."

TWENTY-SIXTH IDYLL

Ino and Autonoa
and apple-cheeked Agava—
these three led three companies
to the mountain. And they picked
wild leaves from the shaggy oaks,
and living ivy, and asphodel—
the kind that grows above ground.
And they built twelve altars
in an open field—three for Semele,
nine for Dionysos. From a chest
they took holy cakes they had made
with their own hands, and reverently
laid them on the new-gathered altars,
just as Dionysos had taught them,
and according to his pleasure.
But from a high rock, Pentheus
spied on everything they were doing,
hidden in a mastic-bush
that grew there. Autonoa
saw him first and gave a terrible cry,
and with her feet quickly scattered
frenzied Bakchos' holy things,
on which the profane do not look.
She herself was in a frenzy,
and immediately the others
became frenzied too. Pentheus
fled in terror, and they pursued,
hitching their skirts above their knees.
Then Pentheus cried out "Women,
what do you mean to do?" Autonoa
shouted "You'll find that out
before there's time for an answer."
The mother seized her son's head
and roared like a lioness
with cubs. Ino set her foot

on his belly and tore off
the great shoulder with the shoulder-blade,
and Autonoa did the same.
The other women tore to pieces
what was left of him, and came
to Thebes, spattered with blood,
bringing down from the mountain
not Pentheus, but penitence.
I care not, for him or anyone
who is Dionysos' enemy—
not even if he should suffer
a worse fate, and be only
nine years old or going on ten.
But for myself, may I be pure
and pleasing to those who are pure,
as the eagle is honored by Zeus,
the aegis-bearer. Good fortune
follows the children of the godly
rather than the ungodly.
Hail Dionysos, whom highest Zeus
set down on snowy Drakanos
when he had opened his mighty thigh.
And hail beautiful Semele
and her sisters, Kadmos' daughters,
honored by all noble women,
who did, at Dionysos' bidding,
this thing which is without blame.
Let no man question the ways of the gods.

TWENTY-SEVENTH IDYLL

Girl.	Another cowherd, Paris, stole prudent Helena.
Daphnis.	But this Helena captures the cowherd with a kiss.
Girl.	Don't brag, young satyr. They say kisses are empty things.
Daphnis.	Yet even in empty kisses there's sweet delight.
Girl.	But see, I wipe my mouth and spit out your kiss.
Daphnis.	You wiped your lips? Let me have them to kiss again.
Girl.	You ought to kiss your cows, not an unmarried girl.
Daphnis.	Don't be so proud. Youth flies quickly by, like a dream.
Girl.	Someday I'll be old, but now I drink milk and honey.
Daphnis.	But grapes turn raisins, and roses wither and die.
Girl.	Let go of me! I'll bite your lips the next time.
Daphnis.	Come here under the olives. I'll tell you something.
Girl.	No, I won't come. I've heard your sweet talk before.
Daphnis.	Then come under these elms and listen to my pipe.
Girl.	Pipe for your own pleasure. I don't like sad music.
Daphnis.	Well, my girl, look out for the Paphian's anger.
Girl.	Forget the Paphian. Artemis protects me.
Daphnis.	Quiet, or she'll strike, and you'll be caught for good.
Girl.	Let her strike if she will. Artemis will defend me.
Daphnis.	You can't escape Eros. No girl ever has.
Girl.	I will, by Pan. But I hope you stay under his yoke.
Daphnis.	I'm afraid he'll give you a worse man than me.
Girl.	Many have wanted me, but none suited my taste.
Daphnis.	Then I too come to join the many who court you.
Girl.	What can I do, friend? Marriage is full of trouble.
Daphnis.	Marriage is neither pain nor sorrow but dancing.

Girl.	Yes, but they say wives are afraid of their husbands.
Daphnis.	The truth is, they always rule them. What have wives to fear?
Girl.	I fear childbirth. Eileithuia's stroke is painful.
Daphnis.	But your queen Artemis helps women in labor.
Girl.	I'm afraid bearing children will spoil my good looks.
Daphnis.	Bear sweet children, and your beauty will shine again.
Girl.	If I say yes, what wedding-gifts will you give me?
Daphnis.	My herds and woodlots and pastures will all be yours.
Girl.	Promise you won't desert me after we're married.
Daphnis.	By Pan I won't, even if you drive me away.
Girl.	Will you build me a bedroom and house and sheep-folds?
Daphnis.	I'll build a bedroom and provide well for your flock.
Girl.	But my gray-haired father, what will I say to him?
Daphnis.	He'll approve your marrying when he hears my name.
Girl.	Say that name of yours. There's often joy in a name.
Daphnis.	I'm Daphnis, son of Lykidas and Nomaia.
Girl.	You come of good family, but mine's as good, I think.
Daphnis.	I know. You're Akrotime. Your father's Menalkas.
Girl.	Show me the woodland where you built your cow-pens.
Daphnis.	Come, then, and see how my slender cypresses grow.
Girl.	Goats, keep on grazing while I see the cowherd's work.
Daphnis.	Feed well, my bulls, while I show the girl my wood-lot.
Girl.	Why do you touch my breasts inside my dress, satyr?
Daphnis.	To teach these early apples of yours they're ripe.
Girl.	I'm fainting, by Pan. Take your hand away again.

Daphnis.   It's all right, dear. Don't be frightened. You're so timid.

Girl.   You've thrown me down by the stream and spoiled my fine clothes.

Daphnis.   But see, I'm putting a soft skin under your dress.

Girl.   You've torn off my girdle. Why are you taking it?

Daphnis.   To be my first offering to the Paphian.

Girl.   Please stop. Somebody's coming. I hear a noise.

Daphnis.   It's the cypresses, whispering of your wedding.

Girl.   You've torn my dress to bits and left me naked.

Daphnis.   I'll give you another one, better than this one.

Girl.   You promise a lot, but soon you'll refuse me salt.

Daphnis.   I wish I could give you my very soul, as well.

Girl.   Artemis, forgive me for breaking my promise.

Daphnis.   I'll give Eros a calf and Aphrodite a cow.

Girl.   I came here a maiden and go home a wife.

Daphnis.   Wife and mother of children, a girl no more.

Delighting in their young bodies, they whispered
to one another, and their secret wedding
was done. She got up and went back to her sheep,
looking ashamed but glad in her heart, and he
went back to his cows, rejoicing in his marriage.

TWENTY-EIGHTH IDYLL

Distaff, spinners' friend, gray-eyed
Athene's gift to women
who cherish the housewife's art,
come boldly along with me
to Neileus' fine city,
where Kypris' shrine is green
among the soft rushes. It's there
we'll sail, praying to Zeus
for fair winds, so I may gladden
my eyes with the sight of my friend
and be welcomed in return
by Nikias, sacred scion
of the sweet-voiced Graces. And you,
my gift of carved ivory,
I'll put in the hands of his wife.
With her you'll make many things—
men's garments, and flowing robes
such as women wear. For twice
each year, if delicate-ankled
Theugenis had her way,
the mothers of lambs in the fields
would be shorn of their soft fleeces,
so busy she is, and so eager
for all that good housewives love.
I wouldn't give you to the house
of a sloven or lazy mistress,
since you come from my own country
and your town is the one Archias
of Ephyra built long ago,
heart of the Trinakrian island—
a city of famous men.
And now you'll dwell in the house
of one who knows all medicines
that ward off painful diseases
from men, in happy Miletos

among the Ionians,
so that Theugenis may boast
of her distaff among the townfolk,
and you will always remind her
of her friend, the lover of songs.
For looking at you, they'll say
"Great love goes with little gifts,
and what comes from a friend is precious."

TWENTY-NINTH IDYLL

There's a saying, "Wine and truth,"
and with this wine, dear boy,
we too must speak the truth,
and I'll tell you what's in my mind:
you don't love me with all your heart.
I know, for I live half my life
in the brightness of your beauty.
But the rest is lost. When you choose,
I spend my day like the gods,
but when you don't, it is dark
indeed. How can it be right
to torment one who loves you?
You're young, and I am older.
Then listen to me, and you'll
be happier, and some day
you'll thank me: make for yourself
one nest in a single tree
where no dangerous, creeping thing
can come. For now you perch one day
on one branch and the next day fly
to another, always seeking
something new. And if a stranger
sees you and praises your pretty face,
you make yourself immediately
a more than three-years' friend to him,
while you put him who loved you first
among your three-day friends.
And you've learned to put on airs
with the great ones. Rather, be true
all your life to your own kind.
That way you'll win great praise
in the town, and never be dealt with
harshly by Eros, that conquers
men's minds easily, and softened
my heart that was once like steel.

By your soft mouth, I beg you
to remember that you were younger
a year ago, and in a moment
we grow wrinkled and gray. We can't
have back our youth, once it's gone,
for youth has winged shoulders,
and we're too slow to catch flying things.
Remembering this, you ought
to be kinder, and return my love,
honestly given, so that when
a man's beard grows on your chin,
we'll be together like Achilles
and his friend. But if you cast
my words to be blown with the winds,
and say in your heart "Good sir,
why do you annoy me?"—though now
I'd fetch you the golden apples,
or Kerberos, keeper of the dead—
why then, even if you stood
at the house-door and called me,
I wouldn't stir, and I'd find
rest from my violent love.

THIRTIETH IDYLL

Alas, I'm sick with grief and pain.
For two months past I've been suffering
from a quartan fever for love of a boy.
He's only moderately good-looking,
but every step he takes is graceful
and his face breaks into sweet smiles.
So far, the fever is with me some days
and goes away again on others,
but soon love will give me no relief,
even for sleeping. Yesterday
he gave me a quick look from under
his eyelids when he passed—too bashful
to look me straight in the face—and blushed.
And love took a tighter grip on my heart
and I went home with fresh, sharp wounds.
Then I called on my soul to listen
and argued a long time with myself:
"What do you think you're doing? And where
do you think this foolishness will get you?
Have you forgotten those three gray hairs
in your head? It's time you had better sense.
You're no longer young in looks and mustn't
behave like one just starting out in life.
And you've forgotten another thing too:
it's better at your age to avoid
the painful love of boys. Life speeds by
like a swift-footed deer. Tomorrow
he'll sail forth on other seas to spend
his young manhood with others his own age.
But memory preys on the lover
and desire feeds on his marrow-bones.
His nights are filled with many dreams,
and a year isn't enough to rid him
of his lovesickness." Such arguments
and many others I presented

to my soul, who answered me thus:
"Whoever hopes to outwit sly love
might just as well try to tell how many
times nine are the stars in the sky.
So whether I like it or not, I stretch
my neck under the yoke and pull,
for that, friend, is the will of the god
who brought down even Zeus's great mind
and the Kypros-born goddess herself.
He lifts me and suddenly sweeps me off
like a quick-withering leaf that needs
no more than a breath of air to stir it."